'COTPA ACT 2003' – SUPREME COURT AND HIGH COURT'S LEADING CASE LAWS

CASE NOTES- FACTS- FINDINGS OF APEX COURT JUDGES & CITATIONS

JAYPRAKASH BANSILAL SOMANI

All the Past & Present Judges of the Supreme Court of India.

Salute to their wisdom.

Salute to their interpretation of Law.

Salute to their elaborative judgement writing.

Supreme Court Of India.

Contents

Contents

Preface

Dear Learned Advocates ofTrial Court, High court and Supreme Court, Corporate and Individuals.

I am very delighted to provide you a book on'COTPA ACT 2003'- SUPREME COURT'S LATEST LEADING CASE LAWs

In this book you will get...

1. Name of the Case i. e. Cause title

2.Relevant Sections discussed in the case

3. Hon'ble Judges/Coram of the case

4.Number of PDF Pages in Original Judgement of the case

5. All available Citations of the case

6. Case Note with appeal allowed/ dismissed or disposed off

7. Facts of the case

8. Hon'ble Apex Court's findings, while dismissing/allowing or disposing the appeal

9. Ratio Decidendi if any.

My special thanks to Manupatra, because of their web portal I can compile this book in well manner. I am also thankful to Notion Press to support me to publish & market this book throughout the Country. Thanks to my Juniors, Advocate Colleagues & Insolvency Professional Colleagues to support me in this venture.

Adv. Manoj Kumar Chowdhary & Miss. Pooja Rai has helped me a lot to compile this book. I hope this book will add some value addition in the wealth of your legal knowledge. Your positive feedbacks will boost me to compile/ write further books & negative feedbacks will improve my skills. Kindly send your valuable feedbacks by email.

Thanks with Regards,

Jayprakash B. Somani

Advocate, Supreme Court of India

Email: jaysomani64@gmail.com

Web Site:www.jayprakashsomani.com

Call: 9322188701, 8459194576

Acknowledgements

Printed & Published by
Notion Press
No. 8, 3rd Cross Street,
CIT Colony, Mylapore,
Chennai, Tamil Nadu- 600004
Managed by
Jayprakash Somani Advocates & Solicitors
Law Firm for Supreme Court of India
Delhi Office
B- 851, 1st Floor, Shivaji Marg, New Ashok Nagar, Delhi 110096.
Call: 9322188701, 8459194576
Supreme Court Chamber
312, 3rd Floor, M. C. Setalvad Block, In front of 'D' Gate, Bhagwan Das
Road, Supreme Court of India, New Delhi 110001
Contact: 8459194576, 9811011747
www.jayprakashsomani.com
Download our app to get access to our Free Videos, Free Bare Acts,
Free Study Material in Legal as well as International Business Regime.
Android App Link ;-https://clpandrea.page.link/cmSm
Ios APp Link :-https://apps.apple.com/us/app/classplus/id1324522260
Login with org code ;- (qywzji)
Web Link ;-https://qywzji.courses.store/
Opportunity for Lawyers/ Social Workers to get Supreme Court Law
Firm JSAS's authorised centre at District Level.
Kindly Message or Call to: 9322188701
Books are available online in India
1.**Notion Press:**https://notionpress.com/author/jayprakash_somani
2.**Amazon:**https://www.amazon.in/s?k=jayprakash+somani
3.**Flipkart:**https://www.flipkart.com/search?q=Jayprakash%20Somani
Books are available online at International Market
4. **Amazon International:** https://www.amazon.com/
s?k=jayprakash+somani
5. **Amazon United Kingdom:** https://www.amazon.co.uk/
s?k=jayprakash+somani

6. E-Books/Kindle edition at National & International Level:
https://www.amazon.in/s?k=jaypraksh+somani

CHAPTER ONE

Shiv Kumar Jatia vs. State of NCT of Delhi (23.08.2019 - SC): MANU/SC/1154/2019

Relative Section:

Cigarettes and other Tobacco Products (Prohibition of Advertisement and Regulation of Trade and Commerce, Production, Supply and Distribution) Act, 2003 - Section 4; Code of Criminal Procedure, 1973 (CrPC) - Section 205, Section 317, Section 482; Indian Penal Code, 1860 (IPC) - Section 32, Section 308, Section 336, Section 338

Hon'bleJudges/Coram:

Abhay Manohar Sapre and R. Subhash Reddy

Equivalent Citation: 2020(206) AIC35, AIR2019SC4463, 2019 (3) ALT (Crl.) 177 (A.P.), 2020CriLJ322, 2019(4)Crimes506(SC), 262(2019)DLT556, 2019/INSC/949, 2019(4)JCC3537, 2019(4)RCR(Criminal)147, 2019(11)SCALE428, (2019)17SCC193, [2019]11SCR210

Case Reference:

Sushil Ansal v. State Through CBI MANU/SC/0190/2014;Sunil Bharti Mittal v. Central Bureau of Investigation MANU/SC/0016/2015;Maksud Saiyed v. State of Gujarat and Ors. MANU/SC/7923/2007;Sharad Kumar Sanghi v. Sangita Rane MANU/SC/0205/2015;Pooja Ravinder Devidasani v. State of Maharashtra MANU/SC/1177/2014; TGN Kumar v. State of Kerala and Ors.MANU/SC/1646/2011;Madan Mohan v. State of Rajasthan and Ors. MANU/SC/1599/2017; State of Haryana and others v. Ch. Bhajan Lal and others MANU/SC/0115/1992

NumberofPagesintheOriginalJudgment: 12

Case Note:

Criminal - Quashing of FIR - Entitlement to - Sections 336, 338 and 32 of Indian Penal Code, 1860 (IPC) and Section 4 of Cigarettes and Other Tobacco Products (Prohibition of Trade and Commerce, Production, Supply and Distribution) Act, 2003 [COTPA, 2003] and Section 482 of Code of Criminal Procedure, 1973 (CrPC) - Present appeals were filed against common judgment passed by High Court opining that, it was not appropriate to quash FIR at Police Station which was registered against Appellants-Accused - Whether impugned FIR was liable to be quashed.

Facts:

The Appellants-Accused have filed criminal misc. cases before the High Court under Section 482 of CrPC seeking quashing of the impugned proceedings including the summoning order passed by the Metropolitan Magistrate. The said petitions are disposed of by the impugned common order by the High Court. High Court has opined that it is not appropriate to quash the FIR which was registered against the Appellants-Accused for offence under Sections 336 and 338 read with Section 32 of IPC and Section 4 of COTPA, 2003.

Held, while allowing the appeals

1. High Court has referred to the contentions in detail and has arrived at the conclusion that it is not a fit case to quash the proceedings. The High Court has mainly relied on the judgment of this Court in the case of Sushil Ansal v. State Through CBI. [22]

2. To prove the alleged offence under Section 336, essential elements are, the act, done rashly and negligently, to endanger human life or personal safety. To prove the guilt of the Accused under Section 338, in addition to the elements under Section 336, an additional consequence of grievous hurt is to be proved. It is clear from the material placed on record that the Appellant (A-4) was not in the country on the date of the incident and the license of the hotel is in the name of Accused No. 3 namely P.R. Subramanian. The owner of the hotel is M/s. Asian Hotels (North) Limited, which is a public listed company made as Accused No. 1. Taking on the face value the allegations made against the Appellant (Accused No. 2) in the chargesheet, so far as Shiv Kumar Jatia, he is sought to be prosecuted for the aforesaid offences only on the ground that he is Managing Director of M/s. Asian Hotels (North) Limited, which runs Hotel Hyatt Regency and also on the ground that he is the only non-independent and Executive Director of the Company who chairs meeting of the company and signatory for various

decisions. [26]

3. Though there are allegations of negligence on the part of hotel and its officers who are incharge of day to day affairs of the hotel, so far as Appellant- Accused No. 2 Shiv Kumar Jatia is concerned, no allegation is made directly attributing negligence with the criminal intent attracting provisions under Sections 336, 338 read with Section 32 of IPC. Taking contents of the final report as it is, present Court is of the view that, there is no reason and justification to proceed against him only on ground that, he was the Managing Director of M/s. Asian Hotels (North) Limited, which runs Hotel Hyatt Regency. The mere fact that he was chairing the meetings of the company and taking decisions, by itself cannot directly link the allegation of negligence with the criminal intent, so far as Appellant- Accused No. 2. 4. By applying the ratio laid down by this Court in the case of Sunil Bharti Mittal, it is clear that, an individual either as a Director or a Managing Director or Chairman of the company can be made an Accused, along with the company, only if there is sufficient material to prove his active role coupled with the criminal intent. Further the criminal intent alleged must have direct nexus with the Accused. [28]

5. Section 4 of the Act prohibits smoking in any public place. However, as per the proviso, a hotel having 30 rooms or a restaurant having seating capacity of 30 persons or more and in the airports, a separate provision for smoking area or space may be made. It is clear that it obligates a hotel having 30 rooms or a restaurant with a seating capacity of 30 persons or more shall have a provision for separate smoking area. In the case on hand, it is merely alleged that though the terrace was not notified as a smoking area, the injured and other resident guests of the hotel were allowed to smoke in the terrace area in the 6th Floor. It is the specific case of the Appellants- Accused that, there is a separate smoking area at the lobby level of the hotel. In absence of making any allegations that hotel has not provided at all any smoking area in the entire hotel, there is absolutely no reason or justification to prosecute the Appellants-Accused for the alleged offence Under Section 4 of COTPA 2003. Even if the allegations are taken on the face value in the chargesheet, no offence is made out against both the Appellants qua the alleged offence committed by them to prosecute under Section 4 of the COTPA 2003. So far as the prosecution Under Section 4 of COTPA 2003 is concerned it is a fit case to be quashed against both the Accused No. 2 - Shiv Kumar Jatia and also Accused No. 4 - Aseem Kapoor. [33]

6. Criminal appeal filed by Shiv Kumar Jatia-Accused No. 2 is allowed by setting aside the order passed by the High Court and consequently criminal proceedings initiated against the Appellant (A-2) and the chargesheet filed in FIR on the file of Police Station at R.K. Puram and further summoning order passed by the learned Metropolitan Magistrate, stands quashed, qua the said Appellant. [37]

7. Criminal appeal filed by the Accused No. 4 - Aseem Kapoor is partly allowed, quashing the chargesheet filed against him in FIR only to the extent of proceedings initiated against him for alleged offence under Section 4 of COTPA 2003. [38]

8. Criminal appeals filed by Ms. Gauari Rishi are dismissed. [39]

CHAPTER TWO

Narinder S. Chadha vs. Municipal Corporation of Greater Mumbai (08.12.2014 - SC) : MANU/SC/1126/2014

Relative Section:

Cigarettes and other Tobacco Products (Prohibition of Advertisement and Regulation of Trade and Commerce, Production, Supply and Distribution) Act, 2003 - Section 2, Section 3,Section 3(1), Section 4,Section 6, Section 7(5), Section 8(2),Section 10, Section 21, Section 24,Section 30, Section 31;

Prevention of Food Adulteration Act, 1954;

Mumbai Municipal Corporation Act, 1888 - Section 394,Section 394(1), Section 479;

Bombay Police Act, 1951 - Section 33;

Code of Criminal Procedure, 1973 (CrPC) - Section 144, Section 144(6);

Prohibition of Smoking in Public Places Rules, 2008 - Rule 2, Rule 3, Rule 3(1),Rule 4, Rule 4(3);

Constitution of India - Article 47 ,

Constitution of India - Article 226,

Constitution of India - Article 366(29A)

Hon'bleJudges/Coram:

Ranjan Gogoi and Rohinton Fali Nariman

Equivalent Citation: 2015(1)ABR807, 2015III AD (S.C.) 131, AIR2015SC756, 2015 (1) ALD(Crl.) 764 (SC), 2015(1)BomCR188, 2015(2)CDR327(SC), 2015(3) CHN (SC) 108, 120(2015)CLT474(SC),

2014/ INSC/ 844, 2015-3-LW693, 2015(I)OLR278, 2014(13)SCALE575, 2015 (1) SCJ 547, [2014]12SCR817

Case Reference: Acts/Rules/Orders:

Narinder S. Chadha and Ors. v. Municipal Corporation of Greater Mumbai and Ors. Civil Appeal Arising out of SLP (C) No. 30832 of 2011; Temperature etc. v. Deputy Police Commissioner, Zone-1 Ahmedabad and Ors. SLP (C) Nos. 19247-19248 of 2012; Robustaa (Hyglow Cafe) v. The Commissioner Corporation of Chennai and Ors. SLP (C) No. 8143 of 2014; Godawat Pan Masala Products I.P. Ltd. and Anr. v. Union of India and Ors. MANU/SC/0574/2004 : (2004) 7 SCC 68; Bajinath Kedia v. State of Bihar and Ors. MANU/SC/0352/1969 : (1969) 3 SCC 838; Paluru Ramakrishnaiah and Ors. v. Union of India and Anr. MANU/SC/0405/1989 : (1989) 2 SCC 541; Northern India Caterers (India) Ltd. v. Lt. Governor of Delhi MANU/SC/0339/1978 : (1979) 1 S.C.R. 557; Electa. B. Merrill v. James W. Hodson 1915 B LRA 481; P. Kasilingam and Ors. v. P.S.G. College of Technology and Ors. MANU/SC/0265/1995 : 1995 Supp (2) SCC 348; Himat Lal K. Shah v. Commissioner of Police, Ahmedabad MANU/SC/ 0583/1972 : (1973) 1 SCC 227

NumberofPagesintheOriginalJudgment: 14

Case Note:

Miscellaneous - Licensed premises - Tobacco products therein - Sale and service thereof - Cigarettes and other Tobacco Products (Prohibition of Advertisement and Regulation of Trade and Commerce, Production, Supply and Distribution) Act, 2003 and Prohibition of Smoking in Public Places Rules, 2008 - High Court disposed of petition in which several wide ranging contentions were urged, and ultimately decided that impugned circular only implemented Cigarettes Act, 2003 and Rules, 2008 and dismissed challenge to said circular - Hence, present appeals - Whether impugned circular travelled outside Cigarettes Act, 2003 and Rules, 2008 or merely seek to implement Cigarettes Act, 2003 and Rules, 2008 as they stood - Held, Cigarettes Act, 2003 was really in implementation of World Health Assembly Resolutions and was enacted to put total ban on advertising of tobacco products and to prevent sale of tobacco products to minors - Unacceptable contention of Municipal Corporation-Respondent that sale of tobacco or tobacco related products would amount to service that could not be so allowed - It was difficult conceptually to say that "sale" and "service" were interchangeable items - If Respondents' contention had to be accepted, Rule 4(3) would be rendered nugatory - What was expressly allowed by

Rule 4(3) could not be said to be taken away by Rule 3(1)(c) - Adding one more exception to two exceptions already contained in Section 6 and it was, thus, clear that this condition would be ultra vires Cigarettes Act, 2003 and Rules, 2008 properly so read - High Court was incorrect when it held that all that Respondent did in present case was to follow Cigarettes Act, 2003 and Rules, 2008 - First paragraph of Condition Number 35 and added words in (C) of Condition Number 35 of impugned circular deleted - Impugned order set aside - Appeals allowed. [paras 8, 12, 13, 19, 21 and 22]

Facts:

1. In this batch of matters, we are concerned with the Municipal Corporations of various cities implementing the Cigarettes and other Tobacco Products (Prohibition of Advertisement and Regulation of Trade and Commerce, Production, Supply and Distribution) Act, 2003. In the first case before us, namely, civil appeal arising out of SLP (C) No. 30832 of 2011 - Narinder S. Chadha and Ors. v. Municipal Corporation of Greater Mumbai and Ors., a judgment of the Bombay High Court dated 11th August, 2011 disposed of a writ petition in which several wide ranging contentions were urged, and ultimately decided that the impugned circular dated 4th July, 2011 only implemented the Cigarettes and other Tobacco Products (Prohibition of Advertisement and Regulation of Trade and Commerce, Production, Supply and Distribution) Act, 2003 (hereinafter referred to as the "Cigarettes Act") and the Prohibition of Smoking in Public Places Rules, 2008 (hereinafter referred to as the "Rules") and dismissed the challenge to the said circular. Similarly, in cases arising from Chennai and Ahmedabad, similar circulars/notices were under challenge and in both the impugned judgments in SLP (C) Nos. 19247-19248 of 2012 (Temperature etc. v. Deputy Police Commissioner, Zone-1 Ahmedabad and Ors.) and SLP (C) No. 8143 of 2014 (Robustaa (Hyglow Cafe) v. The Commissioner Corporation of Chennai and Ors.), the Gujarat and Madras High Courts followed the Bombay High Court judgment dated 11th August, 2011 and, consequently, dismissed the writ petitions filed before them. It is from these three judgments that appeals have been preferred.

From a reading of Himat Lal's case, it is clear that the word "regulate" would not include the power to prohibit. Further, Section 144 of the Code of Criminal Procedure provides a power to grant only temporary orders which cannot last beyond 2 months from the making thereof (see Section 144(6) of the Code of Criminal Procedure). Despite this being pointed out to the High Court, the High Court held:

Held, while allowing the appeals in part

There is no dispute as regards the position of law and we accept the contentions on behalf of the Petitioners so far as Section 144 of the Code is concerned. However, solely on this ground alone the entire action on the part of the Police Commissioner cannot be said to be unlawful or beyond his jurisdiction. Prima facie, we are convinced that the notification invoked Under Section 144 of the Code was issued with a definite idea and the idea was to immediately give true effect to the addition of the condition in respect of licences of persons running eating house/restaurant. It appears that the authorities felt that it would be difficult to stop the activity of providing hookah at eating house/restaurant by solely adding one of the conditions not to provide hookah at a eating house/restaurant. It appears from the affidavit-in-reply filed by the Police Commissioner that with a view to meet with such an emergent situation prevailing in the city and as it was very difficult to keep constant vigilant and monitoring as regards compliance of the condition which was added in the licence, the Police Commissioner thought fit to invoke Section 144 of the Code.

Assuming for a moment that the action of the Police Commissioner of the city of Ahmedabad in issuing the notification in purported exercise of powers Under Section 144 of the Code is not tenable in law by itself would not be sufficient to grant the relief as prayed for by the Petitioners. Though we do not find error in the same but assuming for a moment that it is found to be illegal and invalid, the High Court while exercising its extraordinary jurisdiction there under can refuse to upset it in public interest. It is a settled principle of law that the remedy Under Article 226 of the Constitution of India is discretionary in nature and in a given case even if such action or order challenged in the petition is found to be improper and invalid, the High Court while exercising its extraordinary jurisdiction thereunder can refuse to upset it.

1. We are at a loss to understand the aforesaid reasoning. If Section 144 is to be invoked, the order dated 14th July, 2011 would have expired 2 months thereafter. The High Court went on to state that while administering the law it is to be tempered with equity and if an equitable situation demands, the High Court would fail in its duty if it does not mould relief accordingly. It must never be forgotten that one of the maxims of equity is that 'equity follows the law'. If the law is clear, no notions of equity can substitute the same. We are clearly of the view that the Gujarat High Court judgment dated 2nd December, 2011 deserves to be set aside not only for following the

Bombay High Court judgment impugned in the appeals before us but for the reasons stated hereinabove.

2. All the appeals are allowed in the aforesaid terms. There will be no order as to costs.

Sugandhi Snuff King Pvt. Ltd. and Ors. vs. Commissioner (Food Safety) Government of NCT of Delhi and Ors. (27.09.2022 - DELHC) : MANU/DE/3764/2022

Relative Section:

Central Sales Tax Act, 1956 - Section 14(ix); Cigarettes And Other Tobacco Products (prohibition Of Advertisement And Regulation Of Trade And Commerce, Production, Supply And Distribution) Act, 2003 - Section 10, Section 11, Section 12, Section 13, Section 14, Section 15, Cigarettes And Other Tobacco Products (prohibition Of Advertisement And Regulation Of Trade And Commerce, Production, Supply And Distribution) Act, 2003 - Section 16 Section 29, Section 3(k), Section 3(p) Section 31, Section 4, Section 5, Section 6, Section 7, Section 8, Section 9, Code of Criminal Procedure, 1973 (CrPC) - Section 482; Constitution Of India - Article 14, Article 19, Article 19(1), Article 19(6), Article 21, Article 226,Article 47; Food Safety And Standards Act, 2006 - Section 18, Section 2, Section 2(j), Section 25, Section 26, Section 26(2), Section 27, Section 28, Section 3, Section 3(1),Section 3(j), Section 30, Section 30(2), Section 30(3), Section 30(a), Section 31, Section 31(1), Section 32, Section 33, Section 34, Section 4 to Section 17, Section 43 to 67, Section 89, Section

91, Section 92, Section 92(2), Section 93,Section 94, Section 97,Section 97(1); Industries (development And Regulation) Act, 1951 - Section 3; Mumbai Municipal Corporation Act, 1888 - Section 314; Prevention Of Food Adulteration Act,1954 - Section 16, Section 2(v), Section 22, Section 23, Section 23(1A), Section 24, Section 24(2), Section 25,Section 7,7(iv); Prevention Of Food Adulteration Rules, 1955 - Rule 42

Hon'bleJudges/Coram:

Gaurang Kanth,

Equivalent Citation: 294(2022)DLT180, 20222FAC289

Case Reference:

I.T.C. Limited vs. The Agricultural Produce Market Committee and Ors. MANU/SC/0047/2002; Ishwari Khetan Sugar Mills (P) Ltd. and Ors. vs. State of Uttar Pradesh and Ors. MANU/SC/0069/1980; Synthetics and Chemicals Ltd. and Ors. vs. State of U.P. and Ors. MANU/SC/0595/1989; S. Samuel and Ors. vs. Union of India (UOI) and Ors. MANU/SC/0892/ 2003; Collector of Central Excise, Bombay-I and Ors. vs. Parle Exports (P) Ltd. MANU/SC/0081/1988;Union of India (UOI) vs. Elphinstone Spinning and Weaving Co. Ltd. and Ors. MANU/SC/0019/2001;Kishorebhai Khamanchand Goyal vs. State of Gujarat and Ors. MANU/SC/0851/2003;

Life Insurance Corporation of India and Ors. vs. D.J. Bahadur and Ors. MANU/SC/0305/1980; Godawat Pan Masala Products I.P. Ltd. and Ors. vs. Union of India (UOI) and Ors. MANU/SC/0574/2004; State of Andhra Pradesh and Ors. vs. McDowell and Co. and Ors. MANU/SC/0427/1996; Black Diamond Beverages and Ors. vs. Commercial Tax Officer, Central Section Assessment Wing, Calcutta and Ors. MANU/SC/0879/1997;

P. Kasilingam and Ors. vs. P.S.G. College of Technology and Ors. MANU/ SC/0265/1995; Mahalakshmi Oil Mills vs. State of Andhra Pradesh MANU/ SC/0314/1988;Himat Lal K. Shah vs. Commissioner of Police, Ahmedabad and Ors. MANU/SC/0583/1972;Lakshmanasami Gounder vs. Commissioner of Income Tax, Selvamani and Ors. MANU/SC/0451/ 1992;Jacob Puliyel vs. Union of India (UOI) and Ors. ANU/SC/0566 /2022;D.S. Nakara and Ors. vs. Union of India (UOI) MANU/SC/0237/ 1982; State of Maharashtra vs. Manubhai Pragaji Vashi and Ors. MANU/ SC/0001/1996; Rustom Cavasjee Cooper and Ors. vs. Union of India (UOI) MANU/SC/0011/1970; Manohar Lal vs. State of U.P. MANU/UP/0921/ 1989; Khedan Lal and Sons vs. State of U.P. and Ors. MANU/UP/0376/ 1980; The State of Bombay vs. Virkumar Gulabchand Shah MANU /SC/ 0005/1952;Pyarali K. Tejani vs. Mahadeo Ramchandra Dange and Ors.

MANU/SC/0146/1973; State of Tamil Nadu vs. R. Krishnamurthy MANU/SC/0258/1979; Krishan Gopal Sharma and Ors. vs. Govt. of N.C.T. of Delhi MANU/SC/1162/1996; Bishan Dass Mehta and Ors. vs. Union of India and Ors. MANU/ DE/ 0011 /1970; M. Mohammed vs. Union of India and Ors. MANU/TN/0258/2015; M/s. Dhariwal Industries Limited and another vs. The State of Maharashtra and others MANU/MH/1519/2012; J. Anbazhagan vs. The Union of India and Ors. MANU/TN/2109/2018; Sri Kamadhenu Traders vs. State of Telangana and Ors. MANU /TL/1327/2021; Mohammad Yamin Naeem Mohammad and Ors. vs. The State of Maharashtra and Ors. MANU /MH/ 0024/ 2021; Sanjay Anjay Stores and Ors. vs. The Union of India and Ors. MANU/ WB/0846 / 2017 ; Narpatchand A. Bhandari vs. Shantilal Moolshankar Jani and Ors. MANU/SC/0279/1993;K.H. Nazar vs. Mathew K. Jacob and Ors. MANU/SC/1350/2019; Sakhawat Ali vs. The State of Orissa MANU/SC/0093/1954;

Municipal Corporation of the City of Ahmedabad and Ors. vs. Jan Mohammed Usmanbhai and Ors. MANU/ SC /0099/1986; Akshay N. Patel vs. Reserve Bank of India and Ors. MANU/SC/1187/2021; Chintaman Rao and Ors. vs. State of Madhya Pradesh MANU/SC/0008/1950; Justice K.S. Puttaswamy and Ors. vs. Union of India (UOI) and Ors. MANU/SC/1044/2017; K.P. Sugandh Limited and Ors. vs. State of Chhattisgarh and Ors. MANU/CG/0032/2008; Ram Babu Rastogi & Ors. vs. State through Food Inspector (PFA), Government of NCT of Delhi MANU/DE/7058/2011; Food Inspector vs. Rupesh Jain and Ors. MANU/DE/5556/2017;

Omkar Agency and Ors. vs. The Food Safety and Standards Authority of India and Ors. MANU/BH/0504/2016; Joshy vs. State of Kerala MANU/KE/2254/2012; Dharampal Satyapal Ltd. and Ors. vs. State of Assam and Ors. MANU/GH/0589/2017; Jayavilas Tobacco Traders LLP vs. The Designated Officer, Food Safety and Drugs Control Dept. MANU/TN/2146/2017; E. Sivakumar vs. Union of India (UOI) and Ors. MANU/SC /0591 /2018; Jeetmal Ramesh Kumar vs. The Commissioner, Food Safety and Drug Administration Department and Ors. MANU/TN/2513/2019; Uppara Veerendra and Ors. vs. State of Andhra Pradesh and Ors. MANU/AP/ 1517 / 2021; Olga Tellis and Ors. vs. Bombay Municipal Corporation and Ors. MANU/SC/ 0039/ 1985; C.B. Gautam vs. Union of India (UOI) and Ors. MANU/SC/0673/1992;State of T.N. represented by Secretary, Housing Deptt., Madras vs. K. Sabanayagam and Ors. MANU/SC/0836/1998

NumberofPagesintheOriginalJudgment: 66

Case Note:

Commercial - Pan Masala - Ban of - Section 30(2)(a) of Food Safety and Standards Act, 2006 (FSSA), Regulation 2.3.4 of Food Safety and Standards (Prohibition and Restriction on Sales) Regulations, 2011 (FSSR) - Present petition filed to challenge notifications issued under Regulation 2.3.4 of FSSR read with Section 30(2)(a) of FSSA which sought to prohibit manufacture, storage, distribution or sale of Gutka, Pan Masala, flavoured/ scented tobacco, Kharra and similar products - Whether notifications under challenge need interference - Held, impugned Notifications is beyond scope of powers conferred upon authority concerned by FSSA - Cigarettes and Other Tobacco Products (Prohibition of Advertisement and Regulation of Trade and Commerce, Production, Supply and Distribution) Act, 2003 (COTPA) deals with sale and distribution of scheduled tobacco products - COTPA, being special law, occupies entire field for tobacco and tobacco products and would prevail over FSSA which is general law - No intention of Parliament, ever, to impose absolute ban on manufacture, sale, distribution and storage of tobacco and/or tobacco products - Intention is to regulate trade and commerce of tobacco and tobacco products in accordance with COTPA - Doctrine of implied repeal has no application to present case as FSSA and COTPA occupy different fields - FSSA does not impliedly repeal provisions of COTPA - Tobacco cannot be construed as "food" within meaning of provisions of FSSA - Section 30(2)(a) of FSSA has to be read in consonance with Section 18 of FSSA - Power under Section 30(2)(a) of FSSA is transitory in nature - Commissioner of Food Safety can issue prohibition orders only in emergent circumstances after giving opportunity of being heard to concerned food operator(s) - Impugned Notifications issued by Respondent No. 1 year after year in mechanical manner without following general principles laid down under Sections 18 and 30(2)(a) of FSSA - Same is clear abuse of powers conferred upon him under FSSA - Classification sought to be created between smokeless and smoking tobacco for justifying issuance of impugned Notifications is unconstitutional - Petition allowed. [238]

Facts:

1. One of the main issues in the present writ petitions is the legality of imposition of such ban by issuance of a Notification or an order by an administrative body. However, to clearly understand the subject matter, the history of the enactments/legislations involved needs to be expounded.

2. In 1975, the Union made the first attempt to bring tobacco industry under its control through the Tobacco Board Act. Thereafter, the Cigarettes (Regulations of Production, Supply and Distribution) Act, 1975 ("Cigarettes Act") was enacted with the aim and objective to levy certain restrictions in relation to trade and commerce in, and production, supply and distribution of, cigarettes and tobacco products.

3. In a paradigm shift through Notification bearing No. G.S.R. 852(E) dated 13.06.1986, labelling rule was inserted as Clause (zzz) to Rule 42 in the Prevention of Food Adulteration Rules, 1955. The said clause made it compulsory for every package of chewing tobacco to bear a warning. However, the same was omitted by Notification No. G.S.R. 431(E) : MANU/HFAM/0049/2009 dated 19.06.2009.

4. The Cigarettes and Other Tobacco Products (Prohibition of Advertisement and Regulation of Trade and Commerce, Production, Supply and Distribution) Bill, 2001 was tabled in the Parliament with the intention to enact a comprehensive law on tobacco in public interest and in order to protect public health. The COTPA was enacted to give effect to the principles enshrined in Article 47 of the Constitution of India that the "State shall endeavour to bring about prohibition of the consumption, except for medicinal purpose of intoxicating drinks and of drugs which are injurious to health". Accordingly, COTPA repealed the Cigarettes Act. It received the assent of the President on 18.05.2003 and was published in the Gazette of India on 19.05.2003.

Held by Hon'ble Supreme court

1. Considering the submissions made and documents and judgments relied by the parties and in view of the detailed discussion and reasoning mentioned herein above, this Court is of the considered view that:

(a) The impugned Notifications passed by the Commissioner of Food Safety in view of Regulation 2.3.4 in exercise of powers under Section 30(2)(a), is beyond the scope of powers conferred upon him by the FSSA.

(b) The COTPA is a comprehensive legislation dealing with the sale and distribution of scheduled tobacco products and therefore, occupies the entire field relating to tobacco products. Therefore, the COTPA, being a special law, occupies the entire field for tobacco and tobacco products and would prevail over the FSSA which is a general law.

(c) It has never been the intention of the Parliament to impose an absolute ban on manufacture, sale, distribution and storage of tobacco and/or tobacco products. However, the intention of the Parliament is to regulate the trade and commerce of tobacco and tobacco products in accordance with the COTPA, a Central Act which deals with tobacco industry.

(d) The doctrine of implied repeal has no application to the present case as the FSSA and the COTPA occupy different fields i.e., the former applies to the "food industry" while the latter applies to the "tobacco industry". Therefore, the FSSA does not impliedly repeal the provisions of the COTPA.

(e) Tobacco cannot be construed as "food" within the meaning of the provisions of FSSA.

(f) Section 30(2)(a) of the FSSA has to be read in consonance with Section 18 of the FSSA. The power under Section 30(2)(a) is transitory in nature and the Commissioner of Food Safety can issue prohibition orders only in emergent circumstances after giving an opportunity of being heard to the concerned food operator(s). The impugned Notifications, however, have been issued by Respondent No. 1 year after year in a mechanical manner without following the general principles laid down under Section 18 and 30(2)(a) of the FSSA, which is a clear abuse of the powers conferred upon him under the FSSA.

(g) The classification sought to be created between smokeless and smoking tobacco for justifying the issuance of the impugned Notifications is clearly violative of Article 14 of the Constitution.

2. In light of the aforementioned discussion and reasoning, this Court is of the considered view that while issuing the impugned Notifications, the Respondent No. 1/Commissioner of Food safety exceeded its power and authority in contravention of the powers vested in him under the FSSA and therefore, the said impugned Notifications are hereby quashed and set aside.

3. The present Writ Petitions are allowed in the above terms. All the pending applications are disposed off. No order as to cost.

CHAPTER FOUR

Godawat Pan Masala Products I.P. Ltd. and Ors. vs. Union of India (UOI) and Ors. (02.08.2004 - SC) : MANU/ SC/0574/2004

Relative Section:

Central Sales Tax Act, 1956 - Section 14(ix); Constitution Of India - Article 14,Article 19,Article 19(1)(g),Article 19(6), Article 47; Prevention Of Food Adulteration Act,1954 - Section 10, Section 10(1)(c),Section 2(ia),Section 2(v), Section 2(vi), Section 2(viiia), Section 22A, Section 23, Section 23(1A),Section 23(1A)(f),Section 24, Section 24(1),Section 24(2),Section 24(2)(a), Section 3(p), Section 6, Section 7,Section 7(iv)

Hon'bleJudges/Coram:

K.G. Balakrishnan and B.N. Srikrishna

Equivalent Citation: 2005(1)ACR525(SC), AIR2004SC4057, 2004 (Suppl.) ACC 760, 2004(5) ALLMR(SC) 970, 2005(1)BomCR194, 2004(106(4))BOMLR724, JT2004(6)SC179, (2004)4MLJ67(SC), 2004(4) PL JR 62,2004(3)RCR(Criminal)930, 2004(6)SCALE388, (2004)7SCC68, [2004]Supp(3)SCR239, 2004(2)UC1148, 2004 (2)UJ1449

Case Reference:

Commissioner of Income Tax v. Hindustan Bulk Carriers, MANU/SC/ 1215/2002; C.I.T. Central, Calcutta v. National Taj Traders MANU/SC/ 0310/1979 : (1980) 2 SCR 277; O.P. Singla and Anr. v. Union of India and Ors., MANU/SC/0350/1984; Pukhraj Jain v. Padma Kashyap and Anr., MANU/SC/0208/1990 ; Jivendra Nath Kaul v. Collector/District Magistrate and Anr., MANU/SC/0519/1992; Gandhi Irwin Salt Manufacturers Association v. The Government of Tamil Nadu MANU/TN/0020/1996 : AIR 1996 Mad 109; Deep Chand v. The State of U.P. and Ors. MANU/SC/0023/1959 : (1959) Supp. (2) SCR; Ch. Tika Ramji and Ors. v. The State of U.P. and Ors., MANU/SC/0008/1956; Zaverbhai Amaidas v. The State of Bombay, MANU/SC/0040/1954; State of Orissa v. M.A. Tulloch and Co., MANU/SC/0021/1963; Vijay Kumar Sharma and Ors. v. State of Karnataka and Ors., MANU/SC/0368/1990; U.P. State Electricity Board and Ors. v. Hari Shanker Jain and Ors. MANU/SC/0500/1978 :(1979) 1 SCR 355; Gujarat State Cooperative Land Development Bank Ltd. v. P.R. Manded and Ors. MANU/SC/0508/1979; The LIC of India v. D.J. Bahadur and Ors., MANU/SC/0305/1980; Jain Ink Manufacturing Co. v. LIC of India and Anr., MANU/SC/0478/1980; Prof. Sumer Chand v. Union of India and Ors., MANU/SC/0561/1994; Allahabad Bank v. Canara Bank and Anr., MANU/SC/0262/2000; Pt. Rishikesh and Anr. v. Salma Begum, MANU/SC/0743/1995; State of Karnataka and Anr. v. Shri Ranganatha Reddy and Anr., MANU/SC/0062/1977; B.R. Enterprises and Ors. v. State of U.P. and Ors., MANU/SC/0330/1999; State of A.P. v. National Thermal Power Corporation Ltd. and Ors., MANU/SC/0356/2002; Mohd. Faruk v. State of Madhya Pradesh and Ors., MANU/SC/0046/1969; Khoday Distilleries Ltd. and Ors. v. State of Karnataka and Ors., MANU/SC/0572/1995; Dwarka Prasad Laxmi Narain v. The State of U.P. and Ors., MANU/SC/0030/1954; B.B. Rajwanshi v. State of U.P. and Ors., MANU/SC/0036/1988; Maneka Gandhi v. Union of India, MANU/SC/0133/1978; Kanti Lal Babulal v. H.C. Patel, MANU/SC/0308/1967; Ajay Hasia and Ors. v. Khalid Mujib Sehravardi and Ors., MANU/SC/0498/1980; Delhi Transport Corporation v. D.T.C.Mazdoor Congress and Ors.,MANU/SC/0031/1991; Vaman Raghunath Fallary & Sons and Ors. v. State of Goa and Ors., W.P. No. 131 of 2003; P.N. Krishna Lal and Ors. v. Govt. of Kerala and Anr., MANU/SC/1007/1995; P.K. Tejani v. M.R Dange, MANU/SC/0146/1973; Dineshchandra Jamnadas Gandhi v. State of Gujarat, MANU/SC/0163/1989; Municipal Corporation of Delhi v. Kacheroo Mal, MANU/SC/0171/1975; Good fellow v. Johnson, (1965) 1 AER 941; Union of India and Anr. v. Cynamide India Ltd. and Anr., MANU/SC/0076/1987; State of Tamil Nadu v. K. Sabanayagam and Anr., MANU/SC/0836/1998; Tulsipur Sugar Co. case, MANU/SC/0336/1980

NumberofPagesintheOriginalJudgment:28

Case Note:

Constitution of India - Articles 14 and 19--Prevention of Food Adulteration Act, 1954--Sections 7 (iv) and 23--Cigarettes and other Tobacco Products (Prohibition of Advertisement and Regulation of Trade and Commerce, Production, Supply and Distribution) Act, 2003 (Act 34 of 2003)--Schedule--Pan masala and gutka (pan masala containing tobacoo) -- Ban on manufacture, sale, storage and distribution thereof -- Whether notifications issued by State Food (Health) Authorities of Maharashtra, Andhra Pradesh, Tamil Nadu and Goa under Section 7 (iv) of Prevention of Food Adulteration Act imposing such ban for different periods valid?-- Held, "no"--Impugned notifications quashed as bad in law, illegal and unenforceable against appellants/petitioners.

Facts:

1. Petitioners Nos. 1 to 5 are associations and cooperative societies of arecanut growers, petitioners Nos. 6 and 7 are engaged in the manufacture and sale of pan masala and gutka in the State of Karnataka They are aggrieved by a notification dated 27th February, 2002, issued by the competent officer appointed as Food (Health) Authority for the State of Andhra Pradesh under Section 7(iv) of the Act, by which the sale of all brands of pan masala (containing tobacco) and chewing tobacco/ zarda/ khaini under any brand name was prohibited "in the interest of public health" in the entire state of Andhra Pradesh with immediate effect.

2. The petitioners also challenge another notification dated 19th November, 2001 issued by the Director for Public Health and Preventive Medicine and State Food (Health) Authority, Government of Tamil Nadu, under Section 7(iv) of the Act directing that no person shall himself or by any person on his behalf, manufacture for sale or store, sell or distribute: (i) chewing tobacco; (ii) pan masala; (iii) gutka, containing tobacco in any form or any other ingredients injurious to health, under whatever name or description in the State of Tamil Nadu. This notification is purported to have been issued in the "interest of public health", for a period of five years with effect on and from 19th November, 2001.

3. The third notification which is challenged in the writ petition is the notification dated 23rd July, 2002 issued by the Commissioner of Food and Drug Administration and Food (Health) Authority for the State of Maharashtra. By the said notification, issued purportedly in exercise of the powers under Section 7(iv) of the Act, "in the interest of public health", the

sale of gutka and pan masala, containing tobacco or not containing tobacco, is prohibited for a period of five years effective from 1ˢᵗ August, 2002. The notification directs that "no person shall himself or any person on his behalf shall manufacture for sale or store, sell or distribute gutka or pan masala, containing tobacco or not containing tobacco, by whatever name called.

4. The fourth notification challenged in the writ petition is the notification dated 24ᵗʰ January, 2003 issued by the Directorate of Food and Drugs Administration and Food (Health) Authority for the State of Goa. By this notification, purportedly issued under Section 7(iv) of the Act, the "sale of gutka and pan masala, containing tobacco or not containing tobacco, by whatever name called," is prohibited within the state of Goa and it is directed that "no person shall himself or any person on his behalf, shall manufacture for sale or store, sell or distribute gutka or pan masala, containing tobacco or not containing tobacco, by whatever name called." The prohibition in the notification is made effective from 26ᵗʰ January, 2003.

5. All the four notifications are under challenge.

Held quashing the impugned notifications, the Court held :

1. Section 7 (iv) of the Prevention of Food Adulteration Act, 1954 ('Act' for short) is not an independent source of power for the State authority;

2. The source of power of the State Food (Health) Authority is located only in the valid rules made in exercise of the power under Section 24 of the Act by the State Government, to the extent permitted thereunder ;

3. The power of the Food (Health) Authority under the rules is only of transitory nature and intended to deal with local emergencies and can last only for short period while such emergency lasts ;

4. The power of banning an article of food or an article used as ingredient of food, on the ground that it is injurious to health, belongs appropriately to the Central Government to be exercised in accordance with the rules made under Section 23 of the Act, particularly, sub-section (1A) (f) ;

5. The State Food (Health) Authority has no power to prohibit the manufacture for sale, storage, sale or distribution of any article, whether used as an article or adjunct thereto or not used as food. Such a power can only arise as a result of wider policy decision and emanate from Parliamentary legislation or, at least, by exercise of the powers by the Central Government by framing rules under Section 23 of the Act ;

6. The provisions of the Cigarettes and other Tobacco Products (Prohibition of Advertisement and Regulation of Trade and Commerce, Production, Supply and Distribution) Act, 2003, are directly in conflict with the provisions of Section 7 (iv) of the Prevention of Food Adulteration Act, 1954. The former Act is a special Act intended to deal with tobacco and tobacco products particularly, while the latter enactment is a general enactment. Thus, the Act 34 of 2003 being a special Act, and of later origin, overrides the provisions of Section 7 (iv) of the Prevention of Food Adulteration Act, 1954, with regard to the power to prohibit the sale or manufacture of tobacco products which are listed in the Schedule to the Act 34 of 2003;

7. The impugned notifications are ultra vires the Act and, hence, bad in law ;

8. The impugned notifications are unconstitutional and void as abridging the fundamental rights of the appellants guaranteed under Articles 14 and 19 of the Constitution.

Godfrey Phillips India Ltd. vs. Ajay Kumar (01.04.2008 - SC) : MANU/SC/1765/2008

Relative Section:

Cigarettes And Other Tobacco Products (prohibition Of Advertisement And Regulation Of Trade And Commerce, Production, Supply And Distribution) Act, 2003 - Section 5(1), Section 5(2), Section 5(2)(a); Consumer Protection Act, 1986 - Section 13,Section 13(6), Section 14, Section 14(1)(d)

Hon'bleJudges/Coram:

Dr. Arijit Pasayat and P. Sathasivam

Equivalent Citation: AIR2008SC1828, 2008(3)ALD23(SC), 2008(3)ALLMR(SC)855, 2008 (2) AWC 1845(SC),2008(2)C.P.C.360, 2008 (2) CCC 194 , 2008(2)CLJ(SC)90, 2(2008)CLT886, (2008) 2CompL J185 (SC),(2008)2CompLJ185(SC), II(2008)CPJ5(SC), 2008 (2) CPR 147 , (2008)3GLR2043(SC), [2008 (4) JCR 67(SC)], JT2008(4)SC647, 2008-4-LW10, (2008)5MLJ102(SC), 2008(3)RCR(Civil)534, 2008(6)SCALE38, (2008) 4SCC504, 2008(8)UC748, 2008(1)UJ655

Case Reference:

Bharat Dharma Syndicate v. Harish Chandra MANU/MH/0047/1937; The Union of India v. Pandurang Kashinath More MANU/SC/0396/1961

NumberofPagesintheOriginalJudgment:6

Case Note:

Consumer Protection Act, 1986 - Section 13 (6)--Unfair trade practice-- Complaint in public interest—Advertisement issued by appellant in respect of cigarettes manufactured and sold by it under brand name of "Red and

White"--Advertisement stated "Red and White smokers are one of a kind"--Showing smiling face of actor Akshay Kumar holding a cigarette--Complainant had also filed suit in relation to advertisement--District Forum held that parallel proceedings in District Forum by way of P.I.L. could not be entertained--State Commission affirmed order of District Forum--But National Commission allowed revision and issued certain directions including payment of compensation to complainant--Whether justified?--Held, "no"--In absence of permission under Section 13 (6), not permissible for complainant to represent others--After having recorded that complaint in that manner not entertainable--National Commission could not have passed impugned order--Order of National Commission set aside.

Ratio Decidendi:

"If clause regarding issuance of corrective advertisement was not in existence at the time of issuance of the advertisement then the National commission not empowered to issue such directions."

Facts:

The respondent filed a complaint in respect of an advertisement given by the appellant, alleging unfair trade practices. The advertisement was issued in newspapers and magazines in 1999 for the cigarettes manufactured and sold by it under the brand name of "Red & White" in respect of which the directions have been issued.

The impugned advertisement apart from showing the packet of cigarettes with the aforesaid brand name stated "Red & White smokers are one of a kind". The advertisement also shows the smiling face of actor Akshay Kumar holding a cigarette. It also contains the statutory warning "Cigarette smoking is injurious to health" as well as price of the pack. The complaint was dismissed by the District Forum as the complainant had also filed a suit in relation to the impugned advertisement in the Civil Court. It was therefore held by the District Forum that parallel proceedings in the District Forum by way of Public Interest Litigation could not be entertained. In appeal, the State Commission affirmed the order of the District Forum. Thereafter, complainant withdrew the suit, but filed Revision Petition before the National Commission. The National Commission held that the slogan in the advertisement that "Red & White smokers are one of a kind" showing the image of Akshay Kumar indicated that "smokers of Red & White cigarettes could be super actor performing all the film stunts without duplicates". According to the appellant, no evidence was led in the case by the complainant either with regard to the ability of film star Akshay

Kumar to carry out stunts without duplicate or with regard to the alleged impression created by the impugned advertisement upon the complainant. Interestingly, the complainant admitted that he continues to smoke cigarette for more than two decades. The National Commission held as follows:

The case of the complainant is that smoking of cigarette by Akshay Kumar with the slogans used in advertisement would detract the people from the statutory warning. Seeing comparative size of the letters etc. the statutory warning in our view loses its prominence which is usurped by more prominent and attractive Akshay Kumar et al and is sufficient to detract the attention of the viewers from the statutory warning to the image of Akshay Kumar with the slogan indicating smokers of Red and White cigarette could be super actor performing all the film stunts without duplicates.

This according to the National Commission was sufficient to hold that the impugned advertisement amounted the unfair trade practices. On the basis of the aforesaid finding, the National Commission gave the following directions:

(i) to discontinue forthwith the unfair trade practice of detracting from the statutorily specified warning and not publish any advertisements like Ext. 'R-1' in any language giving any impression that a person who smokes Red and White Cigarette could perform such acts as could be performed by Akshay Kumar in films and thereby detracting from the specified warning; and

(ii) to issue corrective advertisements of equal size in all the newspapers in which advertisements in Hindu & English like Ext. R-1 were published to neutralize the effect of the said impugned misleading advertisements.

(iii) Shri Ajay Kumar, the petitioner, shall be paid a sum of Rs. 20,000/- by way of compensation and Rs. 5,000/- as cost.

Held by Hon'ble Supreme Court

1. Interestingly, there was no allegation or finding of loss or injury caused to the respondent on account of the advertisement issued in 1999. The complainant himself had stated that he was smoking cigarettes for the last two decades. Therefore, the impugned advertisement cannot be said to have affected the complainant and/or caused any loss to him to warrant grant of compensation.

2. Another aspect which needs to be noted is that the complainant had stated in his complaint that he had filed a complaint in public interest and had accepted that the matter was pending before the Civil Court. The District Forum and the State Commission had, therefore, dismissed the complaint of the appellant.

3. It is to be noted that the National Commission itself noted that the respondent was not representing a "Voluntary Consumer Association" registered under the Companies Act, 1956 or under any other law for the time being in force and was not entitled to file a complaint about unfair trade practice to represent other consumers. Having said so, it is not understandable as to how the National Commission even proceeded to deal with the complaint. It also noted that the complainant had not moved any application or obtained any permission under Section 13(6) of the Act and/or no such permission was granted. In the circumstances, it was not permissible for the complainant to represent others. The complainant's case right through was that he was filing a petition in public interest. After having recorded that the complaint in that manner was not entertainable, the National Commission could not have passed the impugned order.

4. Looked at from any angle, the orders of the National Commission are indefensible and are set aside. The appeals are allowed with no order as to costs.

CHAPTER SIX

Relative Section: CIGARETTES AND OTHER TOBACCO PRODUCTMahesh Bhatt and Ors. vs. Union of India (UOI) and Ors. (07.02.2008 - DELHC) : MANU/DE/0185/2008

Relative Section:

CIGARETTES AND OTHER TOBACCO PRODUCTS (PROHIBITION OF ADVERTISEMENT AND REGULATION OF TRADE AND COMMERCE, PRODUCTION, SUPPLY AND DISTRIBUTION) ACT, 2003 - Section 2; Section 3, Section 4, Section 5, Section 7, Section 8, Section 10, Section 30, Section 31;

CONSTITUTION OF INDIA - Article 19, Article 21,Article 25

Hon'bleJudges/Coram:

Mukul Mudgal and Sanjiv Khanna, JJ

Equivalent Citation: 2008BUSLR366 (Del), 147(2008)DLT561

Case Reference:

Abrams v. U.S. 250 US 616; Bennett Coleman and Co. v. Union of India (1972) 2 SCC 788; Breard v. City of Alexandria 341 US 622; Cantewell v. Connecticut (1940) 310 US 296; Denis v. U.S. (1950) 341 U.S. 492;

Dharam Dutt v. Union of India (2004) 1 SCC 712; Dr. Ram Manohar Lohia v. State of Bihar and Anr. (1966) 1 SCR 709; Eskayef v. Commissioner of Income Tax (2000) 6 SCC 451; Godawat Pan Masala Products I.P. Limited v. Union of India (2004) 7 SCC 68; In Re: Noise Pollution (2005) 5 SCC 733; Indian Express Newspapers Bombay Private Limited v. Union of India (1985) 1 SCC 641; Jeffrey Cole Bigelow v. Commonwealth of Virginia; Jilubhai Nanbhai Khachar v. State of Gujarat; Knuller (Publishing, Printing and Promotions) Ltd. v. Director of Public Prosecutions; Lewis J. Valentine v. F.J. Chrestensen; M.H. Devendrappa v. Karnataka State Small Industries Development Corporation (1998) 3 SCC 732; Madhu Limaye v. Sub-Divisional Magistrate (1970) 3 SCC 746; Mr. X v. Hospital Z (1998) 8 SCC 296; Municipal Corporation of Greater Bombay v. Bharat PetroChemical Corporation Limited (2002) 4 SCC 216; Murli Deora v. Union of India (2001) 8 SCC 765; N. Subrahmanyan Chettiar v. Muthuswamy Goundan 1940 FCR 188; P.A. Jacob v. Superintendent of Police, Kottayam and Anr. AIR 1993 Ker. 1; P.N. Krishna Lal v. Govt. of Kerala 1995 Supp (2) SCC 187; Ramesh Yeshwant Prabhoo (Dr) v. Prabhakar Kashinath Kunte (1996) 1 SCC 130; S. Rangarajan v. Jagivan Ram (1989) 2 SCC 574; Sakal Papers v. Union of India A.I.R 1962 SC 305; Secretary, Ministry of Information and Broadcasting v. Cricket Association of Bengal (1995) 5 SCC 161; Superintendent, Central Prison v. Ram Manohar Lohia 1960 (2) SCR 821; Tata Press Limited v. Mahanagar Telephone Nigam Ltd. (1995) 5 SCC 139; Valentine v. Chrestensen; Vijay Kumar Sharma v. State of Karnataka (1990) 2 SCC 562; William B. Cammarano v. United States

NumberofPagesintheOriginalJudgment:29

Case Note:

Constitution - Media and Communication - Constitutional validity of Act of 2003 - Legislative competence - Entry 52 of the Union List in Schedule VII and Article 246 of Constitution of India - Cigarette and Other Tobacco Products (Prohibition of Advertisement and Regulation of Trade and Commerce, Production, Supply and Distribution) Act, 2003 - Cigarettes and Other Tobacco Products Prevention of Advertisements and Regulation of Trade and Commerce, Production, Supply and Distribution Rules, 2005 - Act and Rule challenged by producer of films and television programmes by filing a Writ Petition - Act challenged for its legislative competence - Public health a state subject under Schedule VII cannot be enacted by the union - Held, under Article 246, the Union Government is entitled to enact any legislation in relation to an industry, control of which is declared by the Parliament to be expedient in public interest, as stipulated in Entry 52 of the Union List in Schedule VII - Power to legislate on a subject matter includes power to legislate on an ancillary matter - In the present case, Central Government has legislative competence and authority to enact the Act and the Rules on tobacco industry and its prohibition of advertisement in the films or television programs -Petition disposed of

Constitution - Amended Rules ultra virus the Parent Statute - Section 5(3) of the Cigarette and Other Tobacco Products (Prohibition of Advertisement and Regulation of Trade and Commerce, Production, Supply and Distribution) Act, 2003 - Whether the amended rules which defines the indirect advertisement is ultra virus the parent act - Section 5 prohibits any person from taking part in any advertisement relating to tobacco products - Held, Act seeks to prohibit, direct and indirect, advertisement by the person engaged in production, supply or distribution of cigarettes and also any person having control over the media shall be prohibited from advertising, directly or indirectly, cigarettes or tobacco products - Impugned Rules by definition Clause 2(e) seek to define "indirect advertisement" - Advertisements can be direct or indirect and in media surrogate advertisement or indirect advertisement is often resorted to - Rules seek to effectuate and ensure proper implementation of Section 5 of the Act and cannot be regarded as ultra virus or seeking to go beyond the parent statue - Amended rules upheld as valid

Constitution - Advertisements of Tobacco Products - Right to Freedom of Speech and Expression - Violation of - Act of 2003 and amended rules - Constitutional validity - Cigarette and Other Tobacco Products (Prohibition of Advertisement and Regulation of Trade and Commerce, Production, Supply and Distribution) Act, 2003 - Article 19 (1) (a) and Article 19 (2) of Constitution of India - Whether a citizen has right to advertise, directly or indirectly about tobacco products and if so to what extent commercial advertisements are protected under freedom of speech and expression - Held, a commercial advertisement has an element of trade and commerce and does not fall strictly within the concept of freedom of speech for it is not for propagation of ideas' social, political, economic or furtherance of literature or human thought - Protection under Article 19(1)(a) is limited and subject to the public interest test - Predominant nature and character of the article, picture etc. will determine whether it is a commercial advertisement for use of tobacco product, having no element of free speech or a news item published in public interest for the purpose of disseminating information - Hence, right to advertise, directly or indirectly about tobacco products does not get protection under Article 19(1)(a)

Constitution - Advertisements of Tobacco Products - Right to freedom of speech and expression - Right to life - Reasonable restrictions - Test of - Articles 19(1)(a), 19(2) and 21 of Constitution of India - Cigarette and Other Tobacco Products (Prohibition of Advertisement and Regulation of Trade and Commerce, Production, Supply and Distribution) Act, 2003 - Whether impugned legislations pass the test of Article 19(2) of the Constitution - Held, freedom granted under Article 19(1)(a) can be restricted only in the interest of Public Order, morality, decency and inducement for committing an offence - Impugned Act and the Rules though they strictly do not fall within the ambit of Article 19(2) of the Constitution are intra virus and valid as fundamental right under Article 19(1)(a), it has to be harmoniously construed with Article 21 to advance interest of general public - Freedom of speech and expression under Article 19(1)(a) is protected and preserved along with the right to live a healthy life under Article 21 - Restrictions imposed on electronic media and cinematographic films are reasonable and justified - Restrictions imposed on the print media to prevent publication of brand names, logos of tobacco products are also in larger public interest and to promote Right to Life - Petitions disposed of

Ratio Decidendi:

"If amended Rules seek to effectuate and ensure proper implementation of the provisions of the Act, it cannot be regarded as ultra virus or seeking to go beyond the parent statue."

"Union Government is entitled to enact any legislation in relation to an industry, control of which is declared by the Parliament to be expedient in public interest."

"Commercial advertisements are entitled to limited protection under Article 19(1)(a) of the Constitution and are not expressions protected under Article 19(1)(a)."

"Reasonable Restrictions can be imposed on the print media to prevent publication of brand names, logos of tobacco products in larger public interest and to promote right to life."

"Power to legislate on a subject matter in the entry in any of the lists in Seventh Schedule includes power to legislate on an ancillary matter."

Facts:

The present Writ Petitions challenge the legality and validity of some of the provisions of the Cigarette and Other Tobacco Products (Prohibition of Advertisement and Regulation of Trade and Commerce, Production, Supply and Distribution) Act, 2003 (hereinafter referred to as 'the Act', for short) and the amended Cigarettes and Other Tobacco Products Prevention of Advertisements and Regulation of Trade and Commerce, Production, Supply and Distribution) Rules, 2005 (hereinafter referred to as 'the Rules', for short). It may be noted that Writ Petition (Civil) Nos. 18761/2005 and 23716/2005 titled Mahesh Bhatt v. Union of India was filed in this Court, while other two Writ Petition (Civil) Nos. 7410-11/2006 titled Kasturi and sons v. Union of India and Anr. were initially filed in Madras High Court but later on transferred to this Court, by Order dated 27th March, 2006 passed by the Hon'ble Supreme Court.

3. The petitioner in Writ Petition (Civil) Nos. 18761/2005 and 23716/2005 is a reputed Writer, Director and Producer of films and television programmes. The Writ Petitioner in the other two petitions is engaged in publication of the newspaper 'The Hindu'. Both the petitioners claim that the amended Rules violate Freedom of Speech and Expression guaranteed under Article 19(1)(a) of the Constitution of India and are not protected under Article 19(2). It is the contention of the petitioners that if the amended Rules are upheld, they will gag and stifle the film, electronic and print media from expressing themselves and curtail their freedom to communicate, inform public and portray society as it actually exists. Considerable emphasis is placed upon the fact that business and use of tobacco is legal and is not rest extra commercium. Learned Counsel appearing for Kasturi and Sons had submitted that the restrictions and prohibitions under the Act and as envisaged by the amended Rules would prevent the print media from even disseminating news in public interest and Therefore violate the right to Freedom of Speech and Expression guaranteed by the Constitution. It was urged that the said legislations are not reasonable. The legal contentions and issues raised by the parties have been dealt with and examined by us while giving our reasoning. The respondents, on the other hand, had drawn our attention to the object and purpose behind the amendments, the reason and cause why the Act was enacted. It was accordingly submitted that the Rules as framed are constitutionally valid and Article 19(1)(a) of the Constitution is not violated. To avoid prolixity, we are not reproducing in detail the legal contentions and the issues raised separately.

Held by Hon'ble Supreme Court

Normally we would have not quashed the show cause notice and gone into the merits at this stage, without final decision by the respondents. However, in the present case, as we have heard the learned Counsel for the parties at great length on the question of constitutional validity as well as the show cause notice, Therefore we have decided the issue rather than relegating the petitioner to file a reply and if required, after final decision, challenge the order passed by the Respondents.

1. Our findings may be thus crystallized:

(A) Commercial advertisements are entitled to limited protection under Article 19(1)(a) of the Constitution if they are in public interest. Commercial advertisements of tobacco products are not expressions protected under Article 19(1)(a) of the Constitution. Commercial advertisements will include indirect or surrogate advertisements which promote and encourage use of tobacco products. However, commercial advertisements are different and distinct from news. The purpose and object behind news is to disseminate information, thoughts and ideas. Pre-dominant nature and character of the article, picture, etc, will determine whether it is a commercial advertisement or a news item/picture.

(B). The impugned Act and the Rules though they strictly do not fall within the ambit of Article 19(2) of the Constitution are intra virus and valid as Fundamental Right under Article 19(1)(a) and Right to Life under Article 21 have to be harmoniously construed to advance interest of general public.

(C) Restrictions imposed on electronic media and cinematographic films are reasonable and justified.

(D) Restrictions imposed on the print media to prevent publication of brand names, logos of tobacco products are also in larger public interest and to promote Right to Life. The Rules also provide for constitution of a committee representing diverse voices, interest and groups and Therefore adequate safeguards have been provided to prevent harassment. Individual cases of abuse of powers can always be struck down by Courts.

(E) Show cause notice issued to Kasturi and Sons is quashed for the reasons stated above.

2. The Writ Petitions are accordingly disposed of. In the facts and circumstances of the case there will be no order as to costs.

CHAPTER SEVEN

Mahesh Bhatt vs. Union of India (UOI) and Ors. (07.02.2008 - DELHC) : MANU/DE/2298/2008

Relative Section:

Cigarettes And Other Tobacco Products (prohibition Of Advertisement And Regulation Of Trade And Commerce, Production, Supply And Distribution) Act, 2003 - Section 10, Section 22, Section 3, Section 3 (a), Section 30,Section 31, Section 31 (1), Section 5, Section 7, Section 5B;

Constitution Of India - Article 14,Article 19,Article 19 (1) (a),Article 19 (2),

Hon'bleJudgcs/Coram:

Mukul Mudgal and Sanjiv Khanna,

Equivalent Citation: WP (C) Nos. 18761 and 23716/2005

Case Reference:

Secretary, Ministry of Information and Broadcasting v. CAB MANU/SC/ 0246/1995 : 1995 (2) SCC 161; S. Rangarajan v. P. Jagjeevanram MANU/ SC/0475/1989 : 1989 (2) SCC 574; LIC v. Manubhai Shah MANU/SC/ 0032/1993 : (1992) 3 SCC 637; Sakal Papers (P) Ltd. v. UOI MANU/SC/ 0090/1961 : (1962) 3 SCR 842; Bobby Art International v. Om Pal Singh Hoon MANU/SC/0466/1996 : (1996) 4 SCC 1; Bennet Coleman and Co. v. UOI MANU/SC/0038/1972 :AIR 1973 SC 106; Murli S. Deora v. Union of India MANU /SC/0703/2001 :(2001) 8 SCC 765; K.A. Abbas v. Union of India MANU/SC/0053/1970 :(1970) 2 SCC 780

NumberofPagesintheOriginalJudgment: 14

Case Note:

Constitution - Validity of Rule - Rule 4 of Sub-rule 6 of the Cigarettes and other Tobacco Products (Prohibition of Advertisement and Regulation of Trade and Commerce, Production, Supply and Distribution) Rules, 2004 (amended in 2005) - Petitioner challenged Validity of Rule 6 (4) that no individual or person or character in films and television programmes should display tobacco products or their use - Hence, this Petition - Held, creativity and formation of artistic expression could not be curtailed to extent of banning it as films and television serials could and would reflect reality - If film depicts smoking scene which was hit by restriction, it might reflect life with all its manifestations - Therefore, to put total restriction on scenes of smoking in films and serials punishable when smoking was not banned in Court, was an exercise impermissible under Constitution - As such, blanket ban imposed an wholly unreasonable restriction on freedom of speech and expression manifested by artistic freedom - However, cinema must both reflect good and bad aspects of life - Imagine movie where all was well and every character was moral and obeys laws and was happy and contented - Such script apart from being very boring also necessarily had to be very short - Even epics such as 'Mahabharata' and 'Ramayana' have gambling, kidnapping and deceit and such depictions could not be legitimately prohibited to promote morally idealistic society - It was precisely such inroads into right of freedom of speech and expression that had to be curbed and safeguarded as per Article 19(1)(a) of Constitution and accordingly must be struck down - Hence, Rule 4(6) was quashed and set aside as being ultra vires Section 31 of Act and in any event violative of Article 19(1)(a) of Constitution of India - Petition allowed.

Constitution - Validity of Rule - Rule 4 of Sub-rule 8 of the Cigarettes and other Tobacco Products (Prohibition of Advertisement and Regulation of Trade and Commerce, Production, Supply and Distribution) Rules, 2004 (amended in 2005) - Held, freedom of speech and expression was prominent constituent of democracy - Healthy and fetter free press promotes dissemination of news and views - Healthy democracy was sustained by informing and making aware citizens of conflicting and differing paints of view and any inroads into freedom of speech and expression, and any rules made in form of imposing curbs thereon would violate Article 19(1)(a) of the Constitution - Such curbs were not saved by Article 19(2) of the Constitution - Thus, impugned Rule 4(8) in so far as it proscribes in toto photographs of already telecast events clearly violate not only Article 14 but also hinders unreasonably rights guaranteed under Article 19(1)(a) and was not protected by of Article 19(2) of the Constitution - Hence Rule 4(8) was quashed and set aside as being ultra vires Section 31 of the Act and in any event violative of Articles 14 and 19(1)(a) of the Constitution of India - Petition allowed.

Ratio Decidendi:

"When rules are violates provision of Constitution then it shall not be sustainable."

Facts:

The principal question which this Court is required to address in this writ petition pursuant to the challenge by the petitioner as formulated by Shri Sandeep Sethi, Senior counsel, relates to the constitutional validity of Sub-rule 6 Rule 4 of The Cigarettes and other Tobacco Products (Prohibition of Advertisement and Regulation of Trade and Commerce, Production, Supply and Distribution) Rules, 2004 as amended in 2005 (hereinafter referred to as 'the Rules') framed under The Cigarettes and other Tobacco Products (Prohibition of Advertisement and Regulation of Trade and Commerce, Production, Supply and Distribution) Act, 2003 (hereinafter referred to as 'the Act'). The said amended Rule reads as follows:

(6) No individual or a person or a character in films and television programmes shall display tobacco products or their use:

Provided that this sub-rule shall not apply to-

(a) old Indian films and old television programmes, produced prior to coming into effect of this notification, being screened in a cinema hall or theatre or aired on television;

(b) old foreign films and old television programmes, including dubbed and sub-titled "foreign films" and television programmes, being screened in cinema halls or theatres or aired on television;

(c) Indian or foreign documentaries and health spots displaying use of tobacco products made to clearly and unambiguously reflect the dangers and dire consequences of tobacco use being screened in cinema hall or theatre or aired on television;

(d) live coverage of news, current affairs, interviews, public meetings, sports events, cultural events and the like, being telecast on television whereby there is a purely incidental and completely unintentional coverage of use of tobacco products:

Provided further that the exemptions under Clauses (a), (b), (c) and (d) above shall not extend to display of brands of tobacco products or tobacco product placement in any form:

Provided also that close ups of cigarette packages or tobacco products shall not be permissible and such scenes shall be edited by the producer or distributor or broadcaster prior to screening in cinemas or theatres or airing on television.

Explanation (1).- For the purpose of this sub-rule, all films that receive Central Board of Film certification prior to the effective date of this notification shall be categorized as "old films".

Explanation (2).- For the purpose of this sub-rule, "foreign film" implies "imported" as defined in the Cinematography (Certification) Rules, 1983.

(6A) In case of old Indian and foreign films, the owner or manager of the cinema hall or theatre where the film is being screened shall ensure that anti tobacco health spots of minimum thirty seconds duration each are screened at the beginning, middle and end of the said film. The provisions of this sub-rule shall not apply to Clause (c) of Sub-rule 6.

(6B)(a) In case of old television programmes, it shall be mandatory for the broadcaster to ensure either placement of an anti tobacco health warning as a prominent scroll at the bottom of the television screen during the period of such display or airing of anti tobacco health spots for a period of minimum thirty seconds during the telecast of each television programme of thirty minute duration or less.

(b) In case the television programme is more than thirty minutes further airtime of thirty seconds shall be allocated for each incremental thirty minutes, for telecasting anti tobacco spots.

(c) the minimum duration of each anti tobacco spot shall be not less than fifteen seconds.

(d) The provisions of this sub-rule shall not apply to Clauses (c) and (d) of Sub-rule 6:

Provided that, the anti tobacco health warning scroll shall be legible and readable with font in black colour on white background with the warnings "Smoking causes cancer" or "Smoking kills" for smoking form of tobacco use and "Tobacco causes cancer" or "Tobacco kills" for chewing and other form of tobacco or such other warnings as may be specified by the Central Government, from time to time.

Provided further that, the anti tobacco health warning scrolls or health spots shall be in the same language(s) as used in the film or television programme. In case of dubbed or sub-titled films or television programmes, the scrolls or spots shall be carried in the language of dubbing or sub-titlement.

(7) Sub-rule (6) shall not apply to new Indian or foreign films and television programmes displaying use of tobacco products necessary to represent the smoking of tobacco usage of a real historical figure or for representation of a historical era or classified well known character:

Provided that in very rare cases where there is display or use of tobacco products due to compulsions of the script, they shall be supported by a strong editorial justification:

Provided further that the display of usage of tobacco products in such movies and television programmes under this sub-rule shall be subject to the following safeguards:

(a) Film and television programs depicting tobacco related scenes shall mandatorily be given 'A' Certification. Such films and television programmes may be permitted to be telecast at such timings as are likely to have least viewership from persons below the age of eighteen years.

(b) The films or television programs, which depict such scenes, would have a disclaimer by the concerned actor regarding the ill effects of use of such products. The disclaimer would be shown in the beginning, middle and end of the film.

(c) Whenever such scenes are shown in a film or television programme, an anti tobacco health warning scroll will be continuously displayed on the screen starting a minute before the scene and would be continuously displayed until one minute after the scene.

Provided also that there shall not be any display of brands of tobacco products or tobacco product placement in any form:

Provided also that close-ups of cigarette packages or tobacco products shall not be permissible and such scenes shall be edited by the producer or distributor or broadcaster prior to screening in cinemas or theatres or airing on television.

Explanation (1).- For the purpose of this sub-rule, all films and television programmes that receive Central Board of Film certification after the effective date of this notification shall be categorized as 'new'.

Explanation (2).- For the purpose of this sub-rule, representatives from Ministry of Health and Family Welfare shall also be represented in the Central Board of Film Certification.

Held by Hon'ble Supreme Court

1. The freedom of speech and expression is a prominent constituent of democracy. A healthy and fetter free press promotes dissemination of news and views. A healthy democracy is sustained by informing and making aware the citizens of conflicting and differing paints of view and any inroads into the freedom of speech and expression, and any rules made in the form of imposing curbs thereon would violate Article 19(1)(a) of the Constitution. Such curbs are not saved by Article 19(2) of the Constitution. Accordingly, the impugned Rule 4(8) in so far as it proscribes in toto the photographs of already telecast events clearly violate not only Article 14 but also hinders unreasonably the rights guaranteed under Article 19(1)(a) and is not protected by Sub-clause (2) of Article 19 of the Constitution. Thus, while I concur with the quashing of the show cause notice issued to Kasturi and Sons by my learned brother Sanjiv Khanna, J., I am further unable to sustain the constitutional validity of the Rule 4 Sub Rule 8.

2. Accordingly, the writ petitions are allowed and Rule 4(8) is quashed and set aside as being ultra vires Section 31 of the Act and in any event violative of Articles 14 and 19(1)(a) of the Constitution of India.

CHAPTER EIGHT

Commissioner (Food Safety), GNCTD vs. Sugandhi Snuff King Pvt. Ltd. and Ors. (10.04.2023 - DELHC) : MANU/DE/2325/2023

Relative Section:

Code of Criminal Procedure, 1973 (CrPC) - Section 144; FOOD SAFETY AND STANDARDS ACT, 2006 - Section 30(2)(a), Section 2(v), Section 89,Section 30; CIGARETTES AND OTHER TOBACCO PRODUCTS (PROHIBITION OF ADVERTISEMENT AND REGULATION OF TRADE AND COMMERCE, PRODUCTION, SUPPLY AND DISTRIBUTION) ACT, 2003 - Section 6, Section 7

Hon'bleJudges/Coram:

S.C. Sharma, C.J. and Yashwant Varma, J

Equivalent Citation: 2023/DHC/002375

Case Reference:

Olga Tellis and Ors. vs. Bombay Municipal Corporation and Ors. MANU/SC/0039/1985; C.B. Gautam vs. Union of India (UOI) and Ors. MANU/SC/0673/1992; Godawat Pan Masala Products I.P. Ltd. and Ors. vs. Union of India (UOI) and Ors. MANU/SC/0574/2004; State of T.N. represented by Secretary, Housing Deptt., Madras vs. K. Sabanayagam and Ors. MANU/SC/0836/1998; The State of Bombay vs. Virkumar Gulabchand Shah MANU/SC/0005/1952; Pyarali K. Tejani vs. Mahadeo Ramchandra Dange and

Ors.ANU/SC/0146/1973; State of Tamil Nadu vs. R. Krishnamurthy MANU/SC/0258/1979; Krishan Gopal Sharma and Ors. vs. Govt. of N.C.T. of Delhi MANU/SC/1162/1996; S. Samuel and Ors. vs. Union of India (UOI) and Ors. MANU /SC / 0892 /2003;M/s. Dhariwal Industries Limited and another vs. The State of Maharashtra and others MANU /MH /1519/ 2012; J. Anbazhagan vs. The Union of India and Ors. MANU/TN/2109/ 2018; E. Sivakumar vs. Union of India (UOI) and Ors. MANU/SC/0591/ 2018; Jeetmal Ramesh Kumar vs. The Commissioner, Food Safety and Drug Administration Department and Ors. MANU/TN/2513/2019; Sri Kamadhenu Traders vs. State of Telangana and Ors. MANU/TL/1327/ 2021; Omkar Agency and Ors. vs. The Food Safety and Standards Authority of India and Ors. MANU/BH/0504/2016; Lal Babu Yadav vs. State of Bihar and Ors. MANU /BH/ 1188/2012; Sanjay Anjay Stores and Ors. vs. The Union of India and Ors. MANU/WB/0846/2017;Dharampal Satyapal Ltd. and Ors. vs. State of Assam and Ors. MANU/GH/0589/2017;All Kerala Online Lottery Dealers Association vs. State of Kerala and Ors. MANU/SC/ 1281/2015;Uppara Veerendra and Ors. vs. State of Andhra Pradesh and Ors. MANU/AP/1517/2021; Dasa Shekar vs. The State of A.P. and Ors. MANU/ AP/0989/2021;

Himat Lal K. Shah vs. Commissioner of Police, Ahmedabad and Ors. MANU/SC/0583/1972; Ashoka Marketing Ltd. and Ors. vs. Punjab National Bank and Ors. MANU/SC/0198/1991;Mohammad Yamin Naeem Mohammad and Ors. vs. The State of Maharashtra and Ors. MANU/MH/ 0024/2021; The Designated Officer, The Food Safety and Drugs Control Dept. vs. Jayavilas Tobacco Traders LLP MANU/TN/0263/2023;

Government of Tamil Nadu and Ors. vs. K. Sevanthinatha Pandarasannathi and Ors. MANU/TN/3949/2009;

Naya Bans Sarv Vyapar Association (Regd.) vs. Union of India & Ors. MANU/DE/5485/2012; Varshney General Sales and Anr. vs. State of U.P. and Ors. MANU/UP/0148/1994; Godfrey Phillips India Ltd. and Ors. vs. State of U.P. and Ors. MANU/SC/0051/2005; Khoday Distilleries Ltd. and Ors. vs. State of Karnataka and Ors. MANU/SC/0572/1995; Madras City Wine Merchants' Association and Ors. vs. State of T.N. and Ors. MANU/ SC/0815/1994; Rameshchandra Kachardas Porwal vs. State of Maharashtra MANU/SC/0033/1981;

Cooverjee B. Bharucha vs. The Excise Commissioner and the Chief Commissioner, Ajmer and Ors. MANU/ SC/0010/1954; P.N. Krishna Lal and Ors. vs. Govt. of Kerala and Ors. MANU/SC/1007/1995; Municipal

Corporation, Ujjain and Ors. vs. BVG India Limited and Ors. MANU/SC/ 0412/2018; Union of India (UOI) and Ors. vs. Unicorn Industries MANU/ SC/1291/2019; I.T.C. Limited vs. The Agricultural Produce Market Committee and Ors. MANU/SC/0047/2002; United Provinces vs. Mt. Atiqa Begum and Ors. MANU/ FE/ 0003/1940;Thakur Jagannath Baksh Singh vs. United Provinces MANU/FE/0007/1943; Megh Raj and another vs. Allah Rakhia and others MANU/FE/0009/1947; Ch. Tika Ramji and Ors. vs. The State of Uttar Pradesh and Ors. MANU/SC/0008/1956; The Calcutta Gas Company (Proprietary) Ltd. vs. The State of West Bengal and Ors. MANU/SC/0063/1962; The Belsund Sugar Co. Ltd. vs. The State of Bihar and Ors.ANU/SC/0457/1999; Harakchand Ratanchand Banthia and Ors. vs. Union of India (UOI) and Ors. MANU/SC/0038/1969; Ganga Sugar Corporation Ltd. and Ors. vs. State of Uttar Pradesh and Ors. MANU/SC/ 0397/1979; I.T.C. Ltd. and Ors. vs. State of Karnataka and Ors. MANU/SC/ 0007/1985; State of Orissa vs. M.A. Tulloch and Co. MANU/ SC/ 0021/ 1963; Baijnath Kedia vs. State of Bihar and Ors. MANU/SC/0352/1969; Ishwari Khetan Sugar Mills (P) Ltd. and Ors. vs. State of Uttar Pradesh and Ors. MANU/SC/0069/1980; State of Haryana and Ors. vs. Chanan Mal and Ors. MANU/SC/0073/1976; State of West Bengal vs. Union of India (UOI) MANU/SC/0086/1962;

The Kannan Devan Hills Produce vs. The State of Kerala and Ors. MANU/SC/0543/1972; Ajoy Kumar Banerjee and Ors. vs. Union of India (UOI) and Ors. MANU/SC/0263/1984; The J.K. Cotton Spinning and Weaving Mills Co. Ltd. vs. The State of Uttar Pradesh and Ors. MANU/SC/ 0287/1960; Ram Narain vs. The Simla Banking and Industrial Co. Limited MANU/SC/0003/1956; Dineshchandra Jamnadas Gandhi vs. State of Gujarat and Ors. MANU/SC/0163/1989;Municipal Corporation of Delhi vs. Kacheroo Mal MANU/ SC/ 0171 /1975; Andhra Pradesh Grain and Seed Merchants Association and Ors. vs. Union of India (UOI) and Ors. MANU/ SC/0081/1970; The U.P. State Electricity Board and Ors. vs. Hari Shankar Jain and Ors. MANU/ SC/ 0500 /1978; Acharya Jagdishwaranand Avadhuta and Ors. vs. Commissioner of Police, Calcutta and Ors. MANU /SC/0050/ 1983; Gopi Mohun Mullick vs. Taramoni Chowdhrani MANU/WB/0050/ 1879; Bishessur Chuckerbutty and Ors. vs. Emperor MANU/WB/0247/ 1916; Swaminatha Mudaliar vs. Gopalakrishna Naidu MANU/TN/0192/ 1915; Taturam Sahu vs. The State of Orissa MANU/OR/0039/1953; Sri Ram Das Gaur vs. The City Magistrate, Varanasi MANU/UP/0096/1960; Ram Narain Sah and Ors. vs. Parmeshwar Prasad Sah and Ors. MANU/BH/0136/

1942; Babulal Parate vs. State of Maharashtra and Ors. MANU/SC/0155/1961;

Gulam Abbas and Ors. vs. State of Uttar Pradesh and Ors. MANU/SC/0059/1981; Directorate of Film Festivals and Ors. vs. Gaurav Ashwin Jain and Ors. MANU/SC/1778/2007; Asif Hameed and Ors. vs. State of Jammu and Kashmir and Ors. MANU/SC/0036/1989; Shri Sitaram Sugar Co. Ltd. and Ors. vs. Union of India (UOI) and Ors. MANU/SC/0249/1990; Khoday Distilleries Ltd. and Ors. vs. State of Karnataka and Ors. MANU/ SC/0242/1996; BALCO Employees Union vs. Union of India (UOI) and Ors. MANU/SC/0779/2001;State of Orissa and Ors. vs. Gopinath Dash and Ors. MANU/SC/2387/2005; Akhil Bharat Gosewa Sangh and Ors. vs. State of A.P. and Ors. MANU/SC/1795/2006; Krishnan Kakkanth vs. Government of Kerala and Ors. MANU/ SC/0044/1997; Gupta Sugar Works vs. State of U.P. and Ors. MANU/SC/0069/1987;METROPOLIS THEATER COMPANY et al. vs. CITY OF CHICAGO and Ernest J. Magerstadt MANU/USSC/0080/1913;

Jacob Puliyel vs. Union of India (UOI) and Ors. MANU/SC/0566/2022

NumberofPagesintheOriginalJudgment: 101

Case Note:

Commercial - Manufacture, storage, distribution or sale of tobacco - Ban on - Present appeal filed to challenge impugned judgment passed in petition by which notification prohibiting manufacture, storage, distribution or sale of tobacco, flavoured/scented, or mixed with any of said additives and described as gutka, pan masala, flavoured/scented tobacco, kharra was set aside - Whether impugned judgment calls for interference - Held, appellant adopted impugned measures bearing in mind larger number of users of smokeless tobacco - Same was evidenced from scientific reports - Appellant stood statutorily armed to impose prohibition - Said measures were essentially policy imperatives which appellants appear to have borne in mind while issuing impugned notifications - Court cannot interfere with policy decision unless it is wholly erroneous or manifestly arbitrary - Impugned judgment set aside - Appeal allowed. [176]

Facts:

1. The Ministry of Health and Family Welfare in the Union Government1 together with the Government of National Capital Territory of Delhi2 have preferred the present appeals questioning the correctness of the judgment dated 27 September 2022 rendered by a learned Single Judge of the Court. The judgment came to be rendered on a batch of writ petitions which had assailed the validity of a Notification bearing No. F.1(3)DO-

I/2012/10503-10521 dated 25 March 2015 passed by the Commissioner (Food Safety), GNCTD prohibiting the manufacture, storage, distribution or sale of tobacco, flavoured/scented, or mixed with any of the said additives and described as gutka, pan masala, flavoured/scented tobacco, kharra or otherwise called by any other name in its packaged or unpackaged form and sold either separately or as one composite product in the National Capital Territory.

2. Undisputedly, the aforesaid directive though originally prescribed to prevail for a period of one year from the date of publication of the said original notification had been extended from time to time and supplemented by identical notifications issued over the years. Those notifications shall for the sake of brevity be hereinafter referred to as the "Impugned Notifications". The original notification of 25 March 2015 read as under:-

184. The learned Judge has while allowing the writ petitions also alluded to the principles of implied repeal. However, and as this Court had noted while recording the submissions which were addressed in these appeals, the appellants had never contended before the writ court that COTPA stood impliedly repealed upon promulgation of FSSA. There was thus no necessity of the said observations being rendered. In any case, in light of the conclusions recorded hereinabove, we find no ground to interfere with the ultimate conclusion recorded by the learned Judge in this respect.

185. Mr. Kirtiman Singh, learned CGSC had additionally sought to contend that trade and commerce in tobacco is liable to be viewed as res extra commercium. Mr. Singh had in this connection referred to certain observations as entered in Nava Bans Sar Vyapar Association as well as Health for Millions Trust and Unicorn Industries. However, we find ourselves unable to enter such a declaration bearing in mind the categorical observations as were made by the Supreme Court in Godawat. The relevant passages of Godawat in this respect are extracted hereinbelow:-

"53. Is the consumption of pan masala or gutka (containing tobacco), or for that matter tobacco itself, considered so

3. The writ petitioners had assailed the validity of the aforesaid notification on numerous grounds which have been duly noticed and considered by the learned Single Judge in the impugned judgment. The principal challenge, however, appears to have centered around the provisions of the Cigarettes and Other Tobacco Products (Prohibition of Advertisement and Regulation of Trade and Commerce, Production, Supply

and Distribution) Act, 20033 and which, according to the petitioners, conferred a right upon them to undertake the manufacture, production, sale and distribution of pan masala or any other chewing material having tobacco or gutka as one of its ingredients . The writ petitioners also appear to have contended that the Food Safety and Standards Act, 20064 was not liable to be considered as an enactment empowering the respondents to pass prohibitory orders impeding or impinging upon the rights conferred upon the petitioners by COTPA. The writ petitioners also questioned the validity of the prohibitory orders in light of the 'declaration of expediency' as embodied in COTPA and the expression of public interest of the Union taking under its control the tobacco industry by virtue of Entry-52 falling in List-I of the Seventh Schedule of the Constitution.

4. For the purposes of appreciating the challenge which stood raised before the learned Single Judge, it would be apposite to reproduce the principal arguments and issues which stood framed in the batch of writ petitions. The learned Single Judge had, upon noticing the submissions addressed, identified the principal issues as the following:-

"First one being the "scope of the 'declaration of expediency' relating to the 'Food Industry' under Section 2 of the FSSA. Another question for consideration before this Court is the "trade and commerce in, manufacture of, supply and distribution of Tobacco covered under the term 'Food Industry'".

Held by Hon'ble High Court Delhi

186. Accordingly, and for all the aforesaid reasons, we find ourselves unable to sustain the impugned judgment rendered by the learned Judge. These appeals shall consequently stand allowed. The impugned judgment and order dated 23 September 2022 shall stand set aside.

187. For reasons aforenoted, we find no merit in the challenge raised in W.P.(C) No. 3362/2015. It shall, in consequence, stand dismissed.

CHAPTER NINE

Ram Babu Rastogi and Ors. vs. State (22.12.2011 - DELHC) : MANU/DE/7058/2011

Relative Section:

Cigarettes And Other Tobacco Products (prohibition Of Advertisement And Regulation Of Trade And Commerce, Production, Supply And Distribution) Act, 2003 - Section 3(p); Code of Criminal Procedure, 1973 (CrPC) - Section 482; Prevention Of Food Adulteration Act,1954 - Section 16, Section 2(ix),Section 2(v), Section 7, Section 7(iv)

Hon'bleJudges/Coram:

Hon'ble Mr. Justice M.L. Mehta

Equivalent Citation: 190(2012)DLT348, 2012(1)JCC472

Case Reference:

Sri Krishan Gopal Sharma & Anr. Vs. Govt. of NCT of Delhi, MANU/SC/1162/1996 : 1996 (4) SCC 513;

Pyarali K.Tejani Vs. Mahadeo Ramchandra Dange & Others, MANU/SC/0146/1973 : AIR 1974 SC 228;

Godawat Pan Masala Products I.P.Ltd. and Another Vs. Union of India and Others, 2004 (2) FAC 33;

Nehrudasan Vs. Food Inspector, Madurai Corporation, Madurai, 2010 (1) FAC 49;

A. Rajasingh & Ors. Vs. The Food Inspector, 2008 (1) FAC 172;

T. Prabhu & Another Vs. The State, 2007 (1) FAC 314;

Hindustan Lever Limited and Others Vs. Food Inspector, 2007 (1) FAC 299

NumberofPagesintheOriginalJudgment: 5

Case Note:

Criminal - Quashing of Summon - Section 3(p) of Cigarettes and Other Tobacco Products (Prohibition of Advertisement and Regulation of Trade and Commerce, Production, Supply and Distribution) Act, 2003 (CPT Act), Sections 2(v), 7 and 16 of Prevention of Food Adulteration Act, 1954 and Section 482 of Criminal Procedure Code, 1973 (Cr.PC) - Present petition under Section 482 of Cr.PC challenged the order under which Petitioner was summoned to face trial alleging violation of Sections 7 and 16 of Act - Whether sample article "Flavored Chewing Tobacco" was a food item and so came within provisions of Act - Held, Section 2(v) of Act defines "food" under which only those articles were included which were used as food or drink for human consumption and which ordinarily enter into or were used in composition - As per expert opinion, sample article was "proprietary food" and within ambit of Appendix B of Rules - There was no mention of "Flavored Chewing Tobacco" in Appendix B - As against this, Section 3(p) of Act defines "tobacco products" as products specified in Schedule - "Flavored Chewing Tobacco" finds its place along with other items like Cigarettes, Cigars, Cheroots, Beedis, Hukkah tobacco, snuff, gutka etc - None of items mentioned in Section 3(p) of Act including chewing tobacco could be said to be falling within meaning of "food" under Section 2(v) of Act, since none of these items could be said to be used as food for human consumption, or ordinarily entering into or used in composition - In view of above, no case against Petitioners was made out and hence impugned order of summon as well as complaint were quashed - Petition stands disposed of accordingly

Facts:

2. On 11.4.2008, a sample of "Flavoured Chewing Tobacco" was purchased for analysis from Vijay Krishan Prem S/o Sh. Ram Gopal Sharma of M/s. Dharam Pal Prem Chand Ltd. The said article was found stored for sale and Mr.Vijay Krishan Prem was found vending the article at the time of taking the sample. The sample consisted of 3 original sealed tin having identical label declaration and batch number. The same was reproduced on notice form VI. The sample was divided into three equal parts and then put in one sealed tin as one counterpart of the samples. Each counterpart containing the sample was separately packed, fastened and sealed according to the Act, 1954 and Rules, 1955. The rest of the formalities were completed. One counterpart of the sample was got analyzed from the Public Analyst and the two remaining counterparts of the sample were deposited

with Local Authority in intact condition. On analysis, the P.A. gave opinion that the sample is covered under the "Cigarettes and Other Tobacco Products (Prohibition of Advertisement and Regulation of Trade and Commerce, Production, Supply and Distribution) Act, 2003' (hereinafter referred to as CTP Act, 2003 in short). The sample was also reported as misbranded because the language of best before declaration was not as per Rule 32 (i) of Rules. The sample of "Flavoured Chewing Tobacco" was also reported to be "proprietary food" and the sample on testing, gave positive result for the presence of Nicotine. It was reported that the tobacco being an ingredient and the presence of Nicotine in the sample article "Flavoured Chewing Tobacco" was in violation of Rule 44J and Rule 37A(2)(c) of the Rules, 1955. Thus sample was reported to be adulterated as it contained Nicotine and Tobacco which are injurious to health. It was alleged in the complaint that in view of clear provisions of Act and the Rules, and the findings of the P.A. about the presence of Nicotine and tobacco in the sample, and the sample being so adulterated, the opinion of the Public Analyst regarding the sample being covered under CTP Act, 2003 had no relevance.

3. The learned M.M. took cognizance of the offences and vide the impugned order dated 25.10.2010, issued summoned against the petitioners.

4. The impugned order has been assailed by the petitioners mainly on two grounds. Firstly, the "Flavoured Chewing Tobacco" was not a food item much less a proprietary food and so, the provisions of Act and the Rules were not applicable. It was submitted that the sample item was a tobacco product within the meaning of Section 3(p) of the CTP Act, 2003. Secondly, the sample item was not covered within the Rule 44J and also Rule 37A(2)(c) of the Rules and that there was no misbranding in violation of Rule 32(i) of the Rules, 1955

Held by Hon'ble High Court

16. In another case titled T. Prabhu & Another Vs. The State, 2007 (1) FAC 314 also, the Madras High Court held that though the word "within" stands omitted after 01.09.2011, but by merely adding such word, the customers could not be said to have been misled or misdirected as there was no difference otherwise in the meaning conveyed. In another case titled Hindustan Lever Limited and Others Vs. Food Inspector, 2007 (1) FAC 299, the Madras High Court held similar view on the label which contained the similar word as in the instant case i.e. "best before within 6 months from

date of packaging".

17. In view of the discussion above, I am of the view that no case against the petitioners is made out and hence the impugned order whereby they were summoned is hereby quashed.

18. Petition stands disposed of accordingly.

CHAPTER TEN

World Lung Foundation-South Asia vs. New Delhi Municipal Council and Ors. (03.12.2012 - DELHC) : MANU/DE/6310/2012

Relative Section:

Cigarettes And Other Tobacco Products (prohibition Of Advertisement And Regulation Of Trade And Commerce, Production, Supply And Distribution) Act, 2003 - Section 3(p), Section 4; Constitution Of India - Article 47; Delhi Prohibition Of Smoking And Non-smokers Health Protection Act, 1996 - Section 5

Hon'bleJudges/Coram:

D. Murugesan, C.J. and Rajiv Sahai Endlaw, J.

Equivalent Citation: W.P.(C) 4579/2012 & CM No. 9509/2012

Case Reference: Nil

NumberofPagesintheOriginalJudgment:5

Case Note:

Environment - Non-implementation of provisions - Cigarettes and Other Tobacco Products (Prohibition chof Advertisement and Regulation of Trade and Commerce, Production, Supply and Distribution) Act, 2003 (COTPA); Prohibition of Smoking in Public Places Rules, 2008 (Smoke Free Rules) -

Petitioner was seeking a mandamus to Respondents No. 1 to 5 Municipal Council/Corporation of Delhi to incorporate in licenses granted to Eating Houses and Hookah bars in particular, a condition to comply with COTPA and Smoke Free Rules and a further direction for cancellation of said licenses for violation of COTPA and Smoke Free Rules - Similar directions were sought against other respondents - Held, relief pressed by Petitioner, of banning of non-nicotine / tobacco hookahs also, for reason that under garb thereof COTPA and Rules framed thereudner were being violated, was not only beyond pleadings in Petition but also not capable of adjudication in present proceedings, rather it was for appropriate authorities to check violations - Similarly, other harmful effect and dangers of spreading contagious diseases, were also beyond scope of present Petition - Counsel for Petitioner failed to show any provision of COTPA or Rules framed thereunder, banning charcoal or charcoal products or use of non-tobacco / nicotine hookahs for reason of same being capable of spreading contagious diseases - No municipality in Delhi was directed to incorporate in licenses issued by it to Hotels, Restaurants, Eating Houses and Food Joints etc., a condition requiring such licensees to comply with provisions of COTPA and Rules framed thereudner and with a further condition that breach thereof would entail cancellation of license - Delhi Police which had incorporated such conditions as aforesaid, was directed to continue to incorporate same - Aforesaid would apply to future licenses issued as well as to existing licenses and also to renewal of licenses - Municipalities as well as Delhi Police were directed to, upon finding any violation by any of Hotels, Restaurants, Eating Houses and Food Joints of provisions of COTPA or Rules framed thereunder, immediately in accordance with law, cancel license and take such other steps as might be necessary / required in law - Petition was allowed

Facts:

1. This petition filed in public interest flags the aspect of non-implementation of the provisions of Cigarettes and other Tobacco Products (Prohibition of Advertisement and Regulation of Trade and Commerce, Production, Supply and Distribution) Act, 2003 (COTPA) and the Rules framed thereunder including the Prohibition of Smoking in Public Places Rules, 2008 (Smoke Free Rules). The particular grievance is that Eating Houses which have been granted licenses, also run Hookah Bars in violation of the COTPA and the Smoke Free Rules. The petition seeks a mandamus to the respondents No. 1 to 5 Municipal Council/Corporation of Delhi to

incorporate in the licenses granted to the said Eating Houses, a condition to comply with the COTPA and the Smoke Free Rules and a further direction for cancellation of the said licenses for violation of COTPA and Smoke Free Rules. Similar directions are also sought against respondent No. 6 Ministry of Health and Family Welfare (Department of Health), Government of India, respondent No. 7 Government of National Capital Territory of Delhi (GNCTD) and respondent No. 8 Delhi Police. Action with respect to the Hookah Parlours and Hookah Bars in particular is sought. Notice of the petition was issued. The National Restaurant Association of India (NRAI) applied for impleadment, which was allowed. Counter affidavits have been filed by the respondent No. 1 New Delhi Municipal Council (NDMC), respondent No. 2 North Delhi Municipal Corporation and respondent No. 3 South Delhi Municipal Corporation, respondent No. 7 GNCTD, respondent No. 8 Delhi Police and by respondent No. 9 NRAI to which rejoinders have been filed by the petitioner.

Held by Hon'ble High Court

1. We are of the opinion that the relief now pressed by the petitioner, of banning of non-nicotine/tobacco hookahs also, for the reason that under the garb thereof COTPA and the Rules framed thereunder are being violated, is not only beyond the pleadings in this petition but also not capable of adjudication in these proceedings. It is for the appropriate authorities, upon detecting individual violations, to adjudicate whether the COTPA and the Rules framed thereunder, are being violated or not. Similarly, the reasons given of harmful effect of burning of charcoal or of other dangers from the use of hookahs i.c. of spreading contagious diseases, are also beyond the scope of this petition which is concerned only as aforesaid with enforcement of the COTPA and the Rules framed thereunder. The counsel for the petitioner inspite of our asking, has been unable to show any provision of the COTPA or the Rules framed thereunder, banning charcoal or charcoal products or use of non-tobacco/nicotine hookahs for the reason of the same being capable of spreading contagious diseases. Suffice it is to observe that if the petitioner has any independent right in this regard, it shall be entitled to pursue the same, as this petition is not concerned with the said aspect.

2. After some hearing, the counsel for the Municipalities as well as the counsel for the NRAI state that the petition for the reliefs claimed be allowed. It is the case of NRAI that its members are not violating the provisions of the COTPA or the Rules framed there under and if any

violation is found, the same be proceeded against in accordance with law. It is further his contention that for the same reason, the NRAI has no objection if the conditions for complying with the COTPA and the Rules framed thereunder are incorporated in the license issued to its members including the existing licenses and if it is also made a condition of the license that violation shall entail cancellation of the license.

3. The Delhi Police as aforesaid have already incorporated the said conditions in the licenses issued by it. The counsels for the Municipalities also state that they have no objection to incorporating such conditions in the licenses issued by them to such Eating Houses, Food Joints, Restaurants, and Hotels etc. We accordingly allow this writ petition and:

(i) direct the New Delhi Municipal Council, the North Delhi Municipal Corporation, the South Delhi Municipal Corporation, the East Delhi Municipal Corporation and any other Municipality having jurisdiction in Delhi to incorporate in the licenses issued by it to Hotels, Restaurants, Eating Houses and Food Joints etc., a condition requiring such licensees to comply with the provisions of the COTPA and the Rules framed thereunder and with a further condition that breach thereof shall entail cancellation of the license. The Delhi Police which though had incorporated such conditions as aforesaid, to continue to incorporate the same;

(ii) the aforesaid shall apply to the future licenses issued as well as to the existing licenses and also to the renewal of the licenses;

(iii) we further direct the Municipalities as well as the Delhi Police to, upon finding any violation by any of the Hotels, Restaurants, Eating Houses and Food Joints of the provisions of the COTPA or the Rules framed thereunder, immediately in accordance with law, cancel the license and take such other steps as may be necessary/required in law.

No costs.

Saurabh Sharma and Ors. vs. Sub-Divisional Magistrate (East) and Ors. (07.04.2021 - DELHC) : MANU/DE/0657/2021

Relative Section:

Cigarettes And Other Tobacco Products (prohibition Of Advertisement And Regulation Of Trade And Commerce, Production, Supply And Distribution) Act, 2003 - Section 3; Code of Criminal Procedure, 1973 (CrPC) - Section 133; Section 195; Disaster Management Act, 2005 - Section 22, Section 22(2), Section 24,Section 35 to 38 Epidemic Diseases Act, 1897 - Section 2,Section 2A,Section 3,Section 3(1); Indian Penal Code 1860, (IPC) - Section 188; Narcotic Drugs And Psychotropic Substances Act, 1985 - Section 42

Hon'bleJudges/Coram:

Prathiba M. Singh, J

Equivalent Citation: Equivalent Citation: 2021 (2) CCC 246 , 281(2021)DLT129

Case Reference:

Satvinder Singh and Ors. vs. The State of Bihar MANU/SC/0854/2019; Gaurav Jain vs. Union of India (UOI) and Ors. MANU/SC/0789/1997

NumberofPagesintheOriginalJudgment: 12

Case Note:

Civil - Covid19 - Non-wearing of face masks - Fine for - Present writ petitions filed challenging imposition of fine of Rs. 500/-, on petitioners, for non-wearing of face masks while travelling alone in private car - Whether case made out for quashing fine imposed - Held, in context of pandemic and wearing of face masks being compulsory - All requisite measures have to be taken by authorities for enforcement of same - Interpretation that furthers purpose of prevention of disease and controlling spread of disease will commend with Court rather than opposite - Challans issued by duly authorised officers - Prayer for quashing of challans is thus not sustainable - Petition dismissed. [55]

Disposition:Petition Dismissed

Facts:

1. These are four writ petitions filed challenging the imposition of fine of Rs. 500/-, on the Petitioners, for non-wearing of face masks while travelling alone in a private car. The brief facts of each of the cases are captured below.

2. In W.P.(C) 6595/2020, the Petitioner's case is that he is a practicing advocate for the last 20 years. On 9th September, 2020, at about 11.00 A.M., he was driving a Honda City DL 13CC 1479, and was stopped by the police near Geeta Colony, New Delhi. It is not disputed that he was travelling alone in his car. After the car was stopped, an Executive Magistrate, along with a Police Constable and a Delhi Police Inspector, informed the Petitioner that a fine of Rs. 500/- is being imposed on him for not wearing a mask in a public place. The Petitioner challenged such imposition of fine before the officials, on the ground that since he was travelling alone in his car, the said car does not constitute a public place and would be a private zone. Accordingly, it is prayed that the challan bearing challan no. 2993, dated 9th September, 2020, be quashed and the amount of Rs. 500/- be refunded. In addition, compensation of Rs. 10,00,000/- is sought on the ground of alleged mental harassment publicly caused to the Petitioner.

3. In W.P.(C) 8455/2020, the facts are that the Petitioner is a lawyer who was stated to be on his way to his chambers at Tis Hazari Courts, around 12.00 noon on 9th August, 2020. He was driving his privately owned car, a Maruti Suzuki Swift and was stopped near Aruna Asaf Ali Hospital, Rajpur Road, Civil Lines by the Police. The Petitioner was in his car travelling alone, with his mask hanging on his face, from one of his ears. The case of the Petitioner is that since he was in his car alone, he had not put the face mask on and that he had intended to wear the mask as soon as he stepped out of the car. It is highlighted that the four windows of the

Petitioner's car were closed. When the police official stopped his car, he was informed that the non-wearing of mask by him is in violation of the Delhi Epidemic Diseases (Management of COVID-19) Regulations, 2020 (hereinafter referred to as 'the Regulations of 2020') and a sum of Rs. 500/- was imposed on him as fine. In this petition, apart from quashing of challan bearing challan no. A-22062, dated 9th August, 2020, a declaration is sought to the effect that privately owned cars are private places for the purpose of the Regulations of 2020. Apart from refund of the amount of Rs. 500/- paid by the Petitioner as fine, a compensation of Rs. 5,00,000/- is sought in the present petition for mental harassment.

4. The Petitioner in W.P.(C) 8588/2020 is also a practicing advocate who states that he was crossing Vikas Marg area near Laxmi Nagar Metro Station on 20th August, 2020 in his privately owned car, with all windows of the car closed. However, officials of the Delhi Police stopped his car on the ground that he was not wearing a face mask in his car. Similarly, an amount of Rs. 500/- was imposed on him as fine for violations of the Regulations of 2020. In this case, a direction is sought that the Respondent-Authorities ought not to fine people for not wearing a face mask while in their own car. Refund of Rs. 500/- is sought, along with compensation of an unascertained sum.

5. In W.P.(C) 9408/2020, the Petitioner is a lawyer stated to be practicing at Karkardooma Courts, New Delhi. On 25th October, 2020, he was travelling in his i-10 Grand bearing no. DL8CAE1725, along with his wife and had reached a spot in front of the of D.C. Office, Nand Nagri at about 1.50 P.M. It is stated that a Civil Defence Personnel forced him to stop his car. After the Petitioner's car was stopped, the Civil Defence Personnel, along with a member of the Enforcement Team of SDM, Shahdara, informed him that since he is not wearing a face mask but only a cotton safa/dupatta/ scarf around his mouth and nose, he would be liable to pay a fine of Rs. 500/-. In this petition also, quashing of the challan dated 25th October, 2020 is prayed for. Along with the quashing of the challan, a refund of Rs. 500/- paid as fine is prayed for, as also compensation of Rs. 10,00,000/- for the harassment and insult allegedly caused to the Petitioner, and for alleged misuse of legal provisions to exhort Rs. 500/- from the Petitioner.

6. From the facts of the above four cases, it is clear that in two of the cases, the Petitioners were not wearing any face masks; in one of the cases case, the Petitioner had a mask which was dangling from one of his ears; and, in the fourth case, the Petitioner was not wearing a mask, but was wearing a safa/dupatta/scarf covering his nose and mouth.

7. The questions which arise in these writ petitions are three-fold. First, whether it is compulsory for persons driving alone in their own private cars to wear face masks and the manner in which such masks ought to be worn. Secondly, if as per the various guidelines, orders and notifications issued, the fine imposed on the Petitioners is valid and legal. Thirdly, if any compensation is liable to be granted.

Held by Hon'ble Court

1. In the context of the pandemic and wearing of face masks being compulsory, all requisite measures have to be taken by the authorities for enforcement of the same. An interpretation that furthers the purpose of prevention of the disease and controlling the spread of the disease will commend with the Court rather than the opposite. The challans have been issued by duly authorised officers. The prayer for quashing of the challans is thus not sustainable.

2.This Court would also like to add that all the four Petitioners in these cases, being advocates/lawyers ought to recognise and assist in implementation of measures to contain the pandemic, rather than questioning the same. Advocates as a class, owing to their legal training have a higher duty to show compliance especially in extenuating circumstances such as the pandemic. Wearing of masks cannot be made an ego issue. Compliance by advocates and lawyers would encourage the general public to show greater inclination to comply. The duty of advocates and lawyers is of a greater magnitude, especially in the context of the pandemic for enforcement of directives, measures and guidelines issued under the Epidemic Diseases Act, 1897 and the Disaster Management Act, 2005.

3. In view of the above, this Court does not find any merit in the writ petitions. The petitions are accordingly dismissed.

Philip Morris Products S.A. and Ors. vs. Anil Kumar Singh and Ors. (10.03.2014 - DELHC) : MANU/DE/0618/2014

Relative Section:

Cigarettes And Other Tobacco Products (prohibition Of Advertisement And Regulation Of Trade And Commerce, Production, Supply And Distribution) Act, 2003 - Section 8, Section 9; Code of Civil Procedure, 1908 (CPC) - Order I Rule 10; Order XXII Rule 10; Order XXVI Rule 10; Order XXVI Rule 9; Order XXXIX Rule 1; Order XXXIX Rule 2; Order XXXIX Rule 7; Section 151; Legal Metrology Act, 2009 - Section 36; Trade Marks Act, 1999 (47 Of 1999) - Section 29, Section 29(1), Section 29(6), Section 30, Section 30(3), Section 30(3)(b), Section 30(4)

Hon'bleJudges/Coram:

Vipin Sanghi, J.

Equivalent Citation: 209(2014)DLT1, MIPR2014(1)357

Case Reference:

Ardath Tobacco Company Ltd. vs. Mr. Munna Bhai and Ors. MANU/DE/0005/2009; Disney Enterprises, Inc. vs. Mr. Rajesh Bharti & Ors. MANU/DE/0454/2013; Kapil Wadhwa & Ors. vs. Samsung Electronics Co. Ltd. & Anr. MANU/DE/4894/2012

NumberofPagesintheOriginalJudgment: 13

Case Note:

Trademark - Infringement - Sections 29 and 30 of Trade Marks Act, 1999 (Act) - Whether sale of impugned cigarettes by Defendants amounted to infringement of Plaintiffs' rights

Facts:

This suit, to claim permanent injunction against infringement of trademarks & passing off, delivery up, damages etc. against the defendants, claiming infringement of plaintiffs' trademarks MARLBORO and the ROOF Device (hereinafter referred to as suit trademarks), was originally filed by Philip Morris Products S.A. (hereinafter referred to as the original plaintiff no. 1) and Philip Morris Services India S.A., plaintiff no. 2 herein. Original Plaintiff no. 1, Philip Morris Products S.A., is a company duly organised and existing under the laws of Switzerland having its principal place of business in Switzerland. Plaintiff no. 2, Philip Morris Services India S.A., is an affiliate of original plaintiff no. 1, having its registered office in New Delhi.

2. The plaintiffs claim that their affiliates around the world, collectively referred to as 'PMI', constitute a leading international tobacco company, with their products being sold in approximately 160 countries and at present, producing 7 of the top 20 best selling global cigarette brands. They have 60 cigarette plants across the world and employ around eighty thousand people. Amongst the international brands of cigarettes manufactured by PMI, the best selling brand of cigarette is MARLBORO.

3. The Plaintiffs claim that since 1924 PMI and its predecessors have been manufacturing and selling cigarettes bearing the trademark MARLBORO. In 1955, the MARLBORO Roof Design label mark (the "Roof Device") was adopted and thereafter, a redesigned MARLBORO brand of cigarettes bearing the Roof Device was introduced in the United States in 1955. It is claimed that since 1957, the plaintiffs have been selling cigarette packs bearing the suit trademarks internationally and have expanded at a steady rate over the years. By virtue of extensive use and publicity, the MARLBORO brand of cigarettes with the ROOF Device has acquired immense global goodwill and reputation over the past decades. Further, it is claimed that MARLBORO is the top selling cigarette brand in the world; that it was ranked No. 17 in the list of "Best Global Brands" released by Interbrand in 2009, with a brand value estimated at approximately U.S. $19 billion; and also that it was included in the top 10 brands in the report on "Most valuable Global brands, 2009" issued by Brandz Top.

4. Original plaintiff no. 1 claimed to be the proprietor of the trademark MARLBORO in India in class 34 under Trademark Registration no. 390938 (Registration date: 21 October 1955), at the time of filing of the present suit. Original plaintiff no. 1 also claimed that it held a number of valid & subsisting registrations for trademarks which incorporated its registered trademark MARLBORO. Following are the details thereof:

Held by Hon'ble Court

Held, once goods have been lawfully acquired i.e. purchased in accordance with law of sale and purchase of goods, whether in India or any other country, sale of such goods in India would not infringe registered Trade mark in India. Therefore, importer of grey market goods/person representing him/subsequent purchaser would not be liable for infringement under Section 29 of Act, if imports/subsequent dealings fall under purview of Section 30(3) of Act.Importer/Defendant has to prove that, impugned goods, bearing a particular Trade mark, were placed in any market worldwide by registered proprietor of said Trade mark or with its consent and thereafter, Defendant lawfully acquired them therefrom. Moreover there was no material to indicate that, Defendants acquired impugned goods from market through legitimate sources. It appears from reports of local commissioners that, there exists a chain/network of supply of these infringing products, but legitimacy of source, from where it originates, was not ascertained. Therefore, in circumstances of case, protection of Section 30(3) of Act, was not available to Defendants because they have failed to show that, impugned cigarettes were lawfully acquired by them from market. Thus, sale of the impugned cigarettes by Defendants amounts to infringement of Plaintiffs' rights in suit Trademarks under Section 29(1) read with 29(6) of Act. Consequently, Plaintiffs were entitled to injunctive reliefs. Suit was decreed in favour of Plaintiffs

Ratio Decidendi:

"Once goods have been lawfully acquired i.e. purchased in accordance with law of sale and purchase of goods, whether in India or any other country, sale of such goods in India would not infringe registered Trade mark in India"

CHAPTER THIRTEEN

Pataka Industries Pvt. Ltd. and Ors. vs. Society For Voice of Human Rights and Justice and Ors. (20.07.2010 - DELHC) : MANU/DE/1784/2010

Relative Section:

CIGARETTES AND OTHER TOBACCO PRODUCTS (PROHIBITION OF ADVERTISEMENT AND REGULATION OF TRADE AND COMMERCE, PRODUCTION, SUPPLY AND DISTRIBUTION) ACT, 2003 - Section 8; Section 9, Section 10, Section 20

Hon'bleJudges/Coram:

S.N. Dhingra, J.

Equivalent Citation: Crl. M.C. 380 and 381 of 2010

Case Reference: Nil

NumberofPagesintheOriginalJudgment:2

Case Note:

Criminal - Quashing of proceedings - Offence committed punishable under Section 20 of the Cigarettes and Other Tobacco Products Act, 2003 - Hence, two petitions under Section 482 of the Code of Criminal Procedure, 1973 (Cr.P.C) - Held, It was thus clear that on date when products purchased Rules for putting statutory warning on packaging not come into force - Thus, no offence made out for label not having warning on the date when products purchased by complainant - Complaint and summoning order passed by trial Court quashed - Hence, petitions allowed.

Facts:

1. By these two petitions under Section 482 Cr.P.C. the petitioners have sought quashing of Complaint No. 1429/1/09 filed before the Metropolitan Magistrate, Delhi under Section 20 of the Cigarettes and Other Tobacco Products (Prohibition of Advertisement & Regulation of Trade & Commerce, Production, Supply and Distribution) Act, 2003 for violation of Sections 8, 9 and 10 of the said Act (hereinafter referred to as "the said Act") by the petitioners and for setting aside order of summoning dated 29th August 2009 passed in the complaints.

2. The sole ground urged by the petitioners before this Court for quashing the order is that the complainant allegedly purchased cigarettes/bidies packets from the shop of the petitioners in April, 2009 whereas the Gazette Notification enforcing the Rules under the said Act came into force on 31st May, 2009. Thus, on the date when the products were purchased by the complainant, the Rules under the said Act had not come into force and the offence cognizance of which was taken by the learned MM was not committed.

3. The said Act was enacted in 2003 and Section 8 of the Act provided that every packet/package of cigarette/bidies or any other tobacco products shall have a specified warning on the package displayed in a legible and conspicuous manner. Sub-section 2 provided that the manner of putting warning on the products shall be such as may be specified in the Rules framed under the Act. Though the Act was passed in 2003, the Rules regarding packaging and labeling were framed in 2008 and were published vide GSR-182(E) dated 18th March, 2008 in Gazette of India Part-II. Rule (1) provided that these Rules shall come into force on the date as Central Government may by notification in Gazette appoint. Thus, the rules specifying how warning was to be displayed did not come into force immediately on publication of the Rules. The nature of warning and the mode of warning were specified in the Schedule of the Rules. It was provided that the size of the warning shall be such that it occupies 40% of the principal display area of the package.

4. The petitioners have placed on record notification of 3rd May, 2009 issued under Tobacco Packaging and Labeling Rules, 2008 which prescribed that the Rules shall come into force on 31st May, 2009. In the Notification

itself it is stated that the principal Rules were published on 15th March, 2008 and they were amended on 29th September 2008 and the Rules came into force on 31st May, 2009.

Held by Hon'ble Court

As per the complaint filed by the complainant before the learned MM, the products were purchased by the complainant from the shop of the petitioners on 20th March, 2009. It is thus clear that on the date when the products were purchased, the Rules for putting statutory warning on the packaging had not come into force. The Rules came into 5. force on 30th May, 2009. Thus, no offence was made out for label not having warning on the date when products were purchased by the complainant. I, therefore, consider that these petitions are to be allowed. It is ordered accordingly. The complaint number 1429/1/09 and summoning order dated 29th August 2009 passed by learned MM is hereby quashed.

6. Both petitions stand disposed of in terms of above order.

CHAPTER FOURTEEN

Raj Products vs. State (Govt. of NCT of Delhi) and Ors. (19.10.2010 - DELHC) : MANU/DE/2920/2010

Relative Section:

CIGARETTES AND OTHER TOBACCO PRODUCTS (PROHIBITION OF ADVERTISEMENT AND REGULATION OF TRADE AND COMMERCE, PRODUCTION, SUPPLY AND DISTRIBUTION) ACT, 2003 - Section 13; Section 14, Section 15, Section 17, Section 19

Hon'bleJudges/Coram:

M.C. Garg, J.

Equivalent Citation: F.A.O. No. 61/2010

Case Reference: nil

NumberofPagesintheOriginalJudgment: 5

Case Note:

Civil - Confiscation of Goods - Rule 3(1)(b) of COTP (Packaging and labeling) Rules 2008 - Trial Court allowed Suit filed by Respondent and held that Petitioner was entitled to confiscate seized gutkha pouches as it was not in conformity with Rule 3(1)(b) of Rules 2008 - Thereby, Respondent was given option to pay in lieu of confiscation, costs equal to value of goods confiscated - Hence, this Appeal - Whether, in absence of necessary statutory warning, goods were liable for confiscation - Held, there was necessity to display statutory warning in an area equivalent to 40% of pre-display area of front panel of pouches in terms of amended notification which had not been done - Pouches which was seized were containing tobacco with label as that of 'Rangeela' Gutkha, 'Panmasala' Gutkha - No evidence was led on file by Appellants that goods seized were in process of replacing/refilling in new packages and were not ready for sale - Thus, in absence of necessary statutory warning, goods were liable for confiscation - Appeal dismissed.

Ratio Decidendi:

"Parties shall lead sufficient evidence before Court that goods seized is in process of replacing in new packages so they are not ready for sale."

Facts:

1. M/s Raj Products has filed this appeal under Order 43 of the Code of Civil Procedure (for short 'C.P.C.') r/w Section 151 C.P.C. and Section 19 of the Cigarettes and other Tobacco Products (Prohibition of Advertisement and Regulation of Trade and Commerce, Product Supply and Distribution) Act, 2003 (hereinafter referred to as "the COTP Act") aggrieved of the order dated 18.1.2010 passed by the learned Additional District Judge, Dwarka Courts, New Delhi in Suit No. 34/2009, whereby the learned Additional District Judge has allowed the suit filed by the respondent and has given the following directions:

36. Resultantly it is ordered that the petitioner is entitled to confiscate the seized gutkha pouches as the respondent has admitted that the same were not in conformity with Rule 3(1)(b) of the COTP (Packaging and labeling) Rules 2008. However, in view of Section 15 of the Act, respondent is given an option to pay in lieu of confiscation, costs equal to the value of goods confiscated. In case the respondent exercises such an option within 15 days and pays the costs to the petitioner equal to the value of the goods, the Superdginama given by respondent will be cancelled and respondent would be entitled to make distribution, sale or supply of such packages after getting the specified health warning incorporated on each package.

37. The petition is therefore allowed. Let the file be consigned to record room.

2. Before the Additional District Judge it was the claim of the respondent that the officers of Central Excise Department headed by the Superintendent, Shri Narender Pal, visited the factory premises of the appellant and examined the finished goods and packing material used for making gutkha pouches lying stored in the factory premises.

3. It was claimed that the specified health warning did not occupy 40% of the principal display area of the front panel of the pouches, which were taken into possession by the respondent during the raid conducted at the

premises of the appellant, which is required under Clause (b) of Sub-rule (1) of Rule 3 of the COTP Act as per the amended notification dated 30.05.2009 [G.S.R. 305(E)] issued by the Ministry of Health and Family Welfare vide F. No. 16011/07/2005-PH.

4. It was the case of the respondent that since the finished goods in the form of gutkha pouches as well as plastic material used for gutkha pouches lying with the appellant were not displaying specified health warning occupying 40% of the principal display area of the front panel of the pouches in violation of Rule 3(a) of the said Rules, the goods were seized under Section 13 of COTP Act. The respondent consequently prayed for confiscation of the goods under Section 14 of the COTP Act.

5. The appellant who contested the proceedings before the Additional District Judge took a plea that it was not a case where statutory warning did not exist on the pouches/packages seized by the respondent, but the warning existed on the packages as per Rules prevalent at that time. The new amendment of Rules came into force two-three months before the seizure. The appellant was always following the Rules. Therefore, the appellant has not committed any Act of violation of the aforesaid Act and Rule.

6. However, the submissions made by the appellant were not found favour with the Additional District Judge who held that the COPT (Packaging and labeling) Rules 2008 came into force with effect from 31.05.2009 after their publication in the official gazette. The Trade Notice is internal communication and has no statutory force. Trade notice is not mandatory. The department is under no obligation to send the Trade Notices and no excuse can be taken by a manufacturer that violation of law between the date of coming into force of Rules and intimation of Trade Notice is to be condoned. The appellant is in the trade of manufacturing tobacco products and cannot take a defence that the Rules which were published in the gazette on 03.05.2009 and came into force on 31.05.2009 were unknown to him till 22.09.2009 when the officials of the respondent searched his factory and seized the offending goods. Therefore, the objection of the appellant that the goods be not confiscated as these were seized by the department prior to intimation of Trade Notice to the appellant is rejected.

Held by Hon'ble Court

13. In the present case, there was a necessity to display the statutory warning in an area equivalent to 40% of the pre-display area of the front

panel of the pouches in terms of the amended notification dated 30.05.009, which admittedly has not been done. As per the panchnama, it is very clear that the pouches which have been seized were containing tobacco with label as that of 'Rangeela' Gutkha, 'Panmasala' Gutkha and thus, in the absence of necessary statutory warning, were liable for confiscation. It is a matter of record that no evidence has been led on the file by the appellants that the goods seized were in the process of replacing/refilling in new packages and thus were not ready for sale.

14. As the learned Counsel for the appellant has not argued with regard to the applicability of the notification, which admittedly is dated 30.05.2009 and there is no other issue which requires adjudication by this Court, the appeal filed by the appellant is dismissed with no orders as to costs. Trial court record, if any, be sent back forthwith.

CM No. 3417/2010 (stay) - Dismissed asinfructuous.

CHAPTER FIFTEEN

Institute of Public Health vs. Union of India and Ors. (01.05.2015 - DELHC) : MANU/DE/1393/2015

Relative Section:

Constitution Of India - Article 226

Hon'bleJudges/Coram:

Rajiv Sahai Endlaw, J

Equivalent Citation: 2015VIIIAD(Delhi)116, 220(2015)DLT262

Case Reference:

Narmada Bachao Andolan vs. Union of India and Others MANU/SC/0640/2000

NumberofPagesintheOriginalJudgment: 5

Case Note:

Miscellaneous - Injunction - Entitlement to - Writ Petition filed for direction to Respondents to withdraw their entire participation, any financial or technical assistance from 12th Annual Asia-Pacific Tax Forum and restraining Respondents from participating in conference - Whether Petitioner entitled for injunction - Held, as far as FCTC was concerned, Article 5.3 of guidelines requires to covenanting States to protect its policies from commercial and other vested interests of tobacco industry in accordance with national law - No provision of any law was barring government functionaries from participation in proposed conference - Though government, for its own reasons, may not participate in an event promoting or glamorizing or encouraging consumption of tobacco and tobacco products but it was a matter for decision of government and it could not be said that any government functionary would be violating any law if decides to do so - Proposed conference was not concerned with use of tobacco and tobacco products - Participation of government and government functionaries was in inaugural function only and hardly any in technical sessions of conference - If people of India disapprove of participation of government functionaries in conference, government would face consequences thereof - Such representatives of people were supposed to know and be aware of needs of people and what was good and bad for them - Petition dismissed.[8],[10],[11],[13] and[15]

Facts:

1. This petition under Article 226 of the Constitution of India, filed as a Public Interest Litigation (PIL), seeks, i) a direction to the respondent No. 1 and its ministries and officials to withdraw their entire participation, any financial or technical assistance from the 12th Annual Asia-Pacific Tax Forum from 5th -7th May, 2015 to be co-organized by International Tax and Investment Centre (ITIC) at New Delhi, ii) a restraint against the Ministry of Finance, Ministry of Health and Family Welfare of the Union of India (UOI) and Government of National Capital Territory of Delhi (GNCTD) and their representatives, employees and officers from participating in any manner in the said conference or attending the conference as resource persons, invitees at the inaugural ceremony etc., iii) a direction to the four respondents to adopt and implement code of conduct for public officials, prescribing the standards with which they should comply in their dealings with the tobacco industry.

2. It is the case of the petitioner:

(i) that ITIC is an organization sponsored and controlled by the International Tobacco Industry, having vested interest in promoting tax policies and reforms beneficial to the tobacco industry;

(ii) that as the conference aforesaid will focus on issues related to tax administration reforms in India and impact of tax policies on trade and investment, the participation of the Union Government and its representatives in the event co-organized by tobacco industry and those working to further the interest of the tobacco industry will be violative of Article 5.3 of the Framework Convention on Tobacco Control (FCTC) to which India is a signatory as well as the FCTC Article 5.3 Guidelines;

(iii) that Article 5.3 of FCTC requires parties to protect their public health policies from the commercial and other vested interests of the tobacco industry in accordance with the national law;

(iv) that the Union and the State Governments, under the provisions of the FCTC, cannot interact with the tobacco industry at an industry-sponsored event where government officials will be lobbied to adopt policies antithetical to public health;

(v) that such interactions also conflict with the Union Government's constitutional obligation to improve public health.

Held by Hon'ble Court

13. There is merit in the contention of the counsel for the respondent UOI that the proposed conference is not concerned with the use of tobacco and tobacco products. Even otherwise we find, that the participation of the government and government functionaries is in the inaugural function only and hardly any in the technical sessions of the conference.

14. Supreme Court in Narmada Bachao Andolan Vs. Union of India MANU/SC/0640/2000 : (2000) 10 SCC 664 held that in exercising of its enormous power, the Court should not be called upon or undertake governmental duties or functions; the Courts cannot run the government and the essence of judicial review is a constitutional fundamental; that in matters of policy, the Court will not interfere; when there is a valid law requiring the Government to act in a particular manner, the Court ought not to, without striking down the law, give any direction and which is not in accordance with law not itself act above the law. Similarly, till the petitioner shows that the proposed actions of the Government sought to be restrained are contrary to any law, this Court cannot issue the restraint order. The Court cannot tell the Government how to go about its conduct and business on a day to day basis.

15. We cannot presume that the government functionaries who have consented to participation in the conference have done so mindlessly or without knowing the background of the sponsors of the conference. Moreover, even if they were not aware, the petitioner by making a representation has made them so aware. The petitioner has not been able to invoke any ground in law whereunder we can restrain them from so participating. It cannot be lost sight of that we are a democratic country and where the government, comprising of representatives of people, is answerable to the people for its actions. If at all the people of India disapprove of the participation of the government functionaries in the conference, government will face the consequences thereof. Such representatives of people are supposed to know and be aware of the needs

of the people and what is good and bad for them.

16. We therefore do not find any merit in the petition which is dismissed.

No costs.

CHAPTER SIXTEEN

Health for Millions Trust vs. Union of India (UOI) and Ors. (08.01.2018 - SC) : MANU/ SC/0653/2018

Relative Section:

Cigarettes and Other Tobacco Products (Prohibition of Advertisement and Regulation of Trade and Commerce, Production, Supply and Distribution) Act, 2003; Constitution of India - Article 19(1); Cigarettes and other Tobacco Products (Packaging and Labelling) Rules, 2008 - Rule 3(1), Rule 5; Cigarettes and other Tobacco Products (Packaging and Labelling) (Amendment) Rules, 2014 - Rule 3,Rule 3(1), Rule 5

Hon'bleJudges/Coram:

Dipak Misra, C.J.I., A.M. Khanwilkar and D.Y. Chandrachud

Equivalent Citation: : 2018(1)SCALE147, (2018)14SCC152

NumberofPagesintheOriginalJudgment:8

Case Reference:

Uttar Pradesh and Ors. v. Hirendra Pal Singh and Ors. MANU/SC/1030/ 2010 : (2011) 5 SCC 305;

Firm A.T.B. Mehtab Majid and Co. v. State of Madras and Anr. MANU/ SC/0352/1962 : AIR 1963 SC 928

Case Note:

Civil – Constitutional validity of Change in Rule - CONSTITUTION OF INDIA - Article 19(1)(g), COTP (Packaging and labeling) Rules 3(1)(b) , 3(1)(d), 3(1)(f), 3(1)(h), Rule 5 of COTP (Packaging and labeling) Rules 2008 – SLP for stay ofthe judgment and order passed by the Division Bench of the High Court of Karnataka at Bangalore in a batch of writ petitions, whereby the High Court has struck down the amendment to the Cigarettes and other Tobacco Products (Packaging and Labelling Rules) 2008, ('the 2008 Rules') as amended by the amending Rules of 2014 ('the 2014 Rules').

Facts:

The High Court has struck down the amendment to the Cigarettes and other Tobacco Products (Packaging and Labelling Rules) 2008, ('the 2008 Rules') as amended by the amending Rules of 2014 ('the 2014 Rules'). On a perusal of the judgment and order passed by the High Court, we find that the first opinion states that the Ministry of Health and Family Welfare was not competent to amend the Rules under the allocation of business rules. According to the said opinion, the other Ministries should have been associated before making the amendment.

The other opinion differs with regard to competence, but concurs as far as lack of empirical data is concerned.

We may note here with profit that both the opinions state that the Rules are arbitrary, being unreasonable.[9]

Held by Hon'ble Court

Considering the rivalized submission advanced at the Bar and keeping in view the objects and reasons of the Cigarettes and Other Tobacco Products (Prohibition of Advertisement and Regulation of Trade and Commerce, Production, Supply and Distribution) Act, 2003 and the measures taken by the State, we think it appropriate to direct stay of operation of the judgment and order passed by the High Court of Karnataka. Though a very structural submission has been advanced by the learned Counsel for the Respondents that it will affect their business, we have remained unimpressed by the said proponement as we are inclined to think that health of a citizen has primacy and he or she should be aware of that which can affect or deteriorate the condition of health. We may hasten to add that deterioration may be a milder word and, therefore, in all possibility the expression "destruction of health" is apposite.

CHAPTER SEVENTEEN

D.S. Chewing Product LLP and Ors. vs. Food Safety Officer (13.12.2022 - DELHC) : MANU/DE/5166/2022

Relative Section:

Cigarettes And Other Tobacco Products (prohibition Of Advertisement And Regulation Of Trade And Commerce, Production, Supply And Distribution) Act, 2003 - Section 14, Section 20,Section 3(p); Code of Criminal Procedure, 1973 (CrPC) - Section 200; , Section 482; Food Safety And Standards Act, 2006 - Section 18,,Section 26,. Section 27, , Section 3, . Section 3(1), , Section 30, , Section 30(2), ,Section 42(4),, Section 52, Section 58,Section 59; Prevention Of Food Adulteration Act,1954 - Section 2(v),Section 7(iv); Prevention Of Food Adulteration Rules, 1955 - Rule 44J

Hon'bleJudges/Coram:

Swarana Kanta Sharma,

Equivalent Citation: 2022/DHC/005519, 2022/DHC/005518

NumberofPagesintheOriginalJudgment: 11

Case Reference:

Food Inspector vs. Rupesh Jain and Ors. MANU/DE/5556/2017;

Ram Babu Rastogi & Ors. vs. State through Food Inspector (PFA), Government of NCT of Delhi MANU/DE/7058/2011;

Godawat Pan Masala Products I.P. Ltd. and Ors. vs. Union of India (UOI) and Ors. MANU/SC/0574/2004;

Krishan Gopal Sharma and Ors. vs. Govt. of N.C.T. of Delhi MANU/SC/1162/1996;

Pyarali K. Tejani vs. Mahadeo Ramchandra Dange and Ors. MANU/SC/0146/1973;

Sugandhi Snuff King Pvt. Ltd. and Ors. vs. Commissioner (Food Safety) Government of NCT of Delhi and Ors. MANU/DE/3764/2022

Case Note:

Criminal-Misc. - Petitions under Section 482 of the Code of Criminal Procedure, 1973- Assailing the summoning order dated 03.02.2022 passed by learned Additional Chief Metropolitan Magistrate-01, Patiala House Courts, New Delhi (hereinafter as "Trial Court") in Complaint Case No. 581/2022 filed under Sections 3/26/27/52/58/59 of Food Safety and Standard Act, 2006 (hereinafter as "FSSA, 2006") and the order dated 04.08.2022 passed in Crl. Revision No. 155/2022 passed by learned Additional Sessions Judge-04, Patiala House Courts, New Delhi (hereinafter as "Appellate Court") and for quashing of entire complaint proceeding-product in question is admittedly chewing tobacco, application of FSSA, 2006 is ruled out

Facts:

1. The petitioner no. 1 in Crl.M.C.5210/2022 is the manufacturer of "Royal Zafrani Zarda", a flavoured chewing tobacco product and petitioner no. 2 to 4 are the designated partners of petitioner no.1. Whereas petitioner no. 1 in Crl.M.C.5624/2022 is the seller of "Royal Zafrani Zarda" and petitioner no. 2 is the nominee/operator of petitioner no. 1. Since both the petitions arise out of same set of facts and contentions and the issue before this Court in both the petitions is also common, the same are being decided through this common judgment.

The brief facts pertinent to adjudication of the present matter are as under:

2.1 The Food Safety Officer suspended herein had taken by purchasing, a sample of article "Royal Zafrani Zarda" for analysis under the provisions of The Food Safety and Standards Act, 2006, Rules and Regulations made thereunder, from one Food Business Operator Sh. Suraj Kumar Garg of M/s Shree Sai Enterprises on 04.02.2021. The sample was taken in presence of witness Sh. Suraj Bhan, Field Assistant. Notice in Form VA was prepared at the spot and copy thereof was given to Food Business Operator. Panchnama was also prepared at the spot and all the sample related documents prepared were read over and explained to Food Business Operator.

2.2 One part of the said sample of "Royal Zafrani Zarda" bearing Sample number 849/1053/21/2021 and the Designated Officer Code Number 08/

DO-24/16948 along with one copy of Form VI & another copy of Form VI in a separate sealed envelope having specimen seal impression was sent to the Food Analyst, Govt. of NCT of Delhi for analysis on 05.02.2021. The remaining two counterparts of the sample along with two copies of Form VI in a sealed packet as well as the fourth counterpart of the sample along with one Form VI in a separate sealed packet were deposited with the then Designated Officer, District South, on 05.02.2021. All copies of Form VI bears specimen seal impression of seal used for sealing sample, counterpart.

2.3 A copy of the Food Analyst Report numbered FSS/157/2021, dated 19.02.2021, was also provided to the concerned parties. The petitioners, through their respective replies, had informed the Food Safety Officer that tobacco and tobacco items are not food and not governed by the provision of FSSA, 2006, and are rather covered under the Cigarettes and Other Tobacco Products (Prohibition of Advertisement and Regulation of Trade and Commerce, Production, Supply and Distribution) Act, 2003. Several judgments of different courts dealing with the present issue were also brought to the notice of the Food Safety Officer. A legal opinion was then obtained by the Food Safety Officer from his department, and after after conclusion of the investigation, the entire case file including the statutory documents, Food Analyst's report, and the Food Safety Officer's report was sent by the Designated Officer to Commissioner (Food Safety), Department of Food Safety, Government of NCT of Delhi, who accorded consent under Section 42(4) of FSS Act, 2006 for the prosecution of accused on 28/01/2022.

Held by Hon'ble Supreme Court

Therefore, considering the facts and circumstances of the case and the settled position of law, when the product in question is admittedly chewing tobacco, application of FSSA, 2006 is ruled out. In view thereof, the impugned orders dated 03.02.2022 and 04.08.2022 along with Complaint Case No. 581/2022 and all proceedings there from are quashed.

Philip Morris Products S.A. and Ors. vs. Sameer and Ors. (10.03.2014 - DELHC) : MANU/DE/0615/2014

Relative Section:

Cigarettes And Other Tobacco Products (prohibition Of Advertisement And Regulation Of Trade And Commerce, Production, Supply And Distribution) Act, 2003 - Section 8, Section 9; Code of Civil Procedure, 1908 (CPC) - Order VIII Rule 10; Order XXVI Rule 10; Rule 9;Order XXXIX Rule 1; Rule 2; Rule 7; Code of Civil Procedure, 1908 (CPC) - Section 151; Legal Metrology Act, 2009 - Section 36; Trade Marks Act, 1999 (47 Of 1999) - Section 29,Section 29(1),Section 29(6),Section 30, Section 30(3), Section 30(3)(b), Section 30(4)

Hon'bleJudges/Coram:

Vipin Sanghi, J.

Equivalent Citation: 2014(58) PTC317 (Del)

NumberofPagesintheOriginalJudgment: 12

Case Reference:

Ardath Tobacco Company Ltd. vs. Mr. Munna Bhai and Ors. MANU/DE/0005/2009;

Dr. Reddy's Laboratory Ltd. vs. Reddy Pharmaceuticals Ltd. MANU/DE/3136/2013;

Kapil Wadhwa & Ors. vs. Samsung Electronics Co. Ltd. & Anr. MANU/DE/4894/2012

Case Note:

Civil-IPR- Trade Mark-Permanent injunction against infringement of trademarks & passing off, delivery up, damages etc against the defendants, claiming infringement of plaintiffs' trademarks MARLBORO and the ROOF Device (hereinafter referred to as suit trademarks), was originally filed by Philip Morris Products S.A.

Plaintiff no. 1 claimed to be the proprietor of the trademark MARLBORO in India in class 34 under Trademark Registration no. 390938 (Registration date: 21 October 1955), at the time of filing of the present suit. Original plaintiff no. 1 also claimed that it held a number of valid & subsisting registrations for trademarks which incorporated its registered trademark MARLBORO.

Plaintiffs claim that apart from statutory rights, they also have also acquired common law rights in the suit trademarks. The goodwill in these trademarks is associated exclusively with the PMI, including the plaintiffs and the suit trademarks, as such, serve as source identifiers for PMI's goods in the minds of the adult consuming public.

Facts:

The plaintiffs claim that their affiliates around the world, collectively referred to as 'PMI', constitute a leading international tobacco company, with their products being sold in approximately 160 countries and at present, producing 7 of the top 20 bestselling global cigarette brands. They have 60 cigarette plants across the world and employ around eighty thousand people. Amongst the international brands of cigarettes manufactured by PMI, the bestselling brand of cigarette is MARLBORO.[2]

The Plaintiffs claim that since 1924 PMI and its predecessors have been manufacturing and selling cigarettes bearing the trademark MARLBORO. In 1955, the MARLBORO Roof Design label mark (the "Roof Device") was adopted and thereafter, a redesigned MARLBORO brand of cigarettes bearing the Roof Device was introduced in the United States in 1955. It is claimed that since 1957, the plaintiffs have been selling cigarette packs bearing the suit trademarks internationally and have expanded at a steady rate over the years. By virtue of extensive use and publicity, the MARLBORO brand of cigarettes with the ROOF Device has acquired immense global goodwill and reputation over the past decades. Further, it is claimed that MARLBORO is the top selling cigarette brand in the world; that it was ranked No. 17 in the list of "Best Global Brands" released by Interbrand in 2009, with a brand value estimated at approximately U.S. $19 billion; and also that it was included in the top 10 brands in the report on

"Most valuable Global brands, 2009" issued by Brandz Top.[3]

The plaintiffs submit that sometime in May 2010, it came to their knowledge that various retailers, in the Fort & Colaba area of Mumbai, were indulging in the sale, stocking & distribution of counterfeit as well as grey market versions of Plaintiffs' products (collectively referred to as 'infringing products' by the plaintiffs), both of which, according to the plaintiffs, are unauthorised and violative of the intellectual property rights of the plaintiffs. To ascertain the truth, services of an independent investigation agency known as M/s. Secure Marc were hired the PMI. Consequently, two rounds of purchases were made on 01.06.2010 and 08.07.2010, whereby a total of 23 samples were purchased from 19 retailers. The said samples were then technically analysed. Examination of the first batch of 20 samples, including the samples purchased from defendant nos. 2-5, revealed that they were grey market products which were not meant for sale in India. With regard to the second batch of 3 samples, extensive technical analysis revealed that 2 of the samples, as were purchased from defendant no. 1, were counterfeit versions of the plaintiffs' product. The plaintiffs claim that the defendants are retailers, wholesalers and distributors, collaboratively and actively, engaged in sale & distribution of infringing products involving plaintiffs' trade name and trademarks, which according to the plaintiffs, are obtained by them from common sources. Consequently, the plaintiffs instituted the present suit against the defendants, seeking the following substantive reliefs:[8]

The plaintiffs submit that some of the products as sold by the defendants are grey market products. According to them, these grey market versions of cigarettes are neither intended to be sold in India, nor are the defendants authorized to sell these cigarettes manufactured by the plaintiffs. They violate several packaging and regulatory laws of the country. Plaintiffs submit that said goods are being sold in violation of Sections 8 & 9 of the Cigarette and Other Tobacco Products (Prohibition of Advertisement and Regulation of Trade & Commerce, Production, supply and Distribution) Act, 2003 read with the relevant provisions of the Cigarette and Other Tobacco Products (Packaging and Labelling) Rules, 2008. Further, the said Cigarettes were also bereft of the proper packaging and labelling prescribed under the Legal Metrology Act, 2009 for the import, sale, distribution and advertising of any product. The said cigarettes contain incorrect Maximum Retail Price labels, and incorrect languages which are not recognised in India. Such sales are in violation of Section 36 of the Legal Metrology Act,

2009 read with Rule 6 of the Legal Metrology (Packaged Commodities) Rules, 2011. Therefore, the plaintiffs submit that even though the smuggled cigarettes may be fit for sale in the country of origin, the same constitute infringing goods in India, as the same differ in packaging, quality, the prescribed tar content, warning labels etc from the genuine products sold in India. In this context, counsel of the plaintiffs has relied upon the case of Societe Des Produits Nestle SA v. Casa Helvetia, Inc., 982 F.2d 633 where the US Federal Court held that "an unauthorized importation may well turn an otherwise "genuine" product into a "counterfeit"". He submits that section 29(1) of the Act does not distinguish between unauthorised sale of genuine or counterfeit goods, but merely states that any unauthorised use of a registered trademark itself will amount to infringement. Hence, import & sale in India, of the said unfit & impaired goods, bearing the suit trademarks, which are in gross violation of the laws of the land and without plaintiffs' authorization, would amount to infringement under Section 29(1) read with section 29(6) of the Act.[15]

Held by Hon'ble Court

The court observed that the defendants being small vendors and not having contested the suit, the plaintiffs had fairly pressed for nominal damages. Court, granting permanent injunction against defendant nos. 1-3, had awarded punitive damages of 25,000/- against each of the said defendant. On the aspect of damages, present case stands on a similar footing as Ardath Tobacco Company (supra). The defendants in question are small/temporary roadside pan shops without any books of accounts or godowns where huge quantities of infringing material could be stocked. In my view, interest of justice would be served in the present case by granting permanent injunction along with awarding nominal damages against the said defendants. Accordingly the suit is decreed in favour of the plaintiffs and against defendant no. 1, 2 &4 in terms of prayers (i), (ii), (iii) & (v) made therein. The plaintiffs are also entitled to the damages of Rs. 10,000 against defendant no. 1 and Rs. 5,000 against each of the other two defendants, in addition to the costs of the suit to be borne by the said defendants equally.

CHAPTER NINETEEN

Naya Bans Sarv Vyapar Association vs. Union of India and Ors. (09.11.2012 - DELHC) : MANU/DE/5485/2012

Relative Section:

Constitution Of India - Article 14, Article 19(1) (g),Article 19(6), Article 37,Article 47

Hon'bleJudges/Coram:

Hon'ble D. Murugesan, Chief Justice and Mr. Justice Rajiv Sahai Endlaw

Equivalent Citation: 20131AD (Delhi) 601, 195(2012) DLT348, 2013(1)ESC62(Del)

NumberofPagesintheOriginalJudgment: 8

Case Reference:

Godawat Pan Masala Products I.P. Ltd. and Anr. vs. Union of India (UOI) and Ors. MANU/SC/0574/2004; Anuj Garg and Ors. vs. Hotel Association of India and Ors. MANU/SC/8173/2007; Public Services Tribunal Bar Association vs. State of U.P. and Anr. MANU/SC/0062/2003; State of Punjab and Anr. vs. Devans Modern Brewaries Ltd. and Anr. MANU/SC/ 0961/2003; World Lung Foundation South Asia vs. Ministry of Health & Family Welfare MANU/DE/2692/2012; Varshney General Sales and Anr. vs. State of U.P. and Ors. MANU/UP/0148/1994; Godfrey Phillips India Ltd. and Anr. vs. State of U.P. and Ors. MANU/SC/0051/2005; Khoday

Distilleries Ltd. and Ors. vs. State of Karnataka and Ors. MANU/SC/0572/1995; Madras City Wine Merchants' Association and Anr. vs. State of T.N. and Anr. MANU/SC/0815/1994; Rameshchandra Kachardas Porwal vs. State of Maharashtra MANU/SC/0033/1981; Cooverjee B. Bharucha vs. The Excise Commissioner and the Chief Commissioner, Ajmer and Ors. MANU/SC/0010/1954; P.N. Krishna Lal and Ors. vs. Govt. of Kerala and Anr. MANU/SC/1007/1995; State of Kerala vs. Kumari T.P. Roshana and Anr. MANU/SC/0051/1979; Jalan Trading Co. (Private Ltd.) vs. Mill Mazdoor Union MANU/SC/0185/1966; State of Madras vs. V.G. Row MANU/SC/0013/1952; Jyoti Pershad vs. The Administrator for The Union Territory of Delhi MANU/SC/0079/1961; The U.P. State Electricity Board and Anr. vs. Hari Shankar Jain and Ors. MANU/SC/0500/1978; R.K. Garg and Ors. vs. Union of India (UOI) and Ors. MANU/SC/0074/1981

Case Note:

Commercial - CONSTITUTION OF INDIA - Article 19(1)(g) - The petitioner, an Association of whole sellers of tobacco and tobacco products, having their shops/establishments at Naya Bans area at Fatehpuri, Chandni Chowk, Delhi,

The cause of action for the petitions accrued to the petitioners when in enforcement of the aforesaid Acts, notices were issued to the members of the petitioner Association to stop carrying on their business aforesaid from their establishments within the prohibited radius of educational institutions.

The counsel for the UOI in his written submissions has urged that the presence of a wholesale shop near educational institution will not only increase the propensity and susceptibility of minors to tobacco products but also in large quantities; that if a distinction were to be made out between whole sellers and retailers, it would lead to a spate of litigation on whether a particular shop is carrying on wholesale or retail sale of tobacco or tobacco products; that the laws aforesaid have been enacted pursuant to the resolution passed in the 39th and 43rd World Health Assembly to inter alia ensure effective protection to non-smokers from involuntary exposure to tobacco smoke and to protect children and young people from being addicted to the use of tobacco which is injurious to health; and lastly that, these are beneficial legislations enacted in the interest of public at large.

Facts:

1. The petitioner, an Association of whole sellers of tobacco and tobacco products, having their shops/establishments at Naya Bans area at Fatehpuri,

Chandni Chowk, Delhi, has instituted these two petitions challenging the provisions of the Cigarettes and Other Tobacco Products (Prohibition of Advertisement & Regulation of Trade and Commerce, Production, Supply and Distribution) Act, 2003 (COTPA) and of the Delhi Prohibition of Smoking and Non-smokers Health Protection Act, 1996 (Prohibition Act) respectively, to the extent they prohibit even wholesale of cigarette(s) or any other tobacco products within a radius of 100 yards of any educational institution, on the following grounds:

(i) that the said market at Naya Bans is the only wholesale market of tobacco and tobacco products in Delhi and in existence since the year 1925;

(ii) that the members of the petitioner Association have been carrying on the wholesale business in tobacco for generations;

(iii) that the customers of the members of the petitioner Association are the large and small retailers, distributors etc. from all over India, who make bulk purchases and who in turn either sell the products to the end-users themselves or through other retailers-the end-users of the product never approach the said market as small quantity or open/loose packets are not sold therein;

(iv) that the members of the petitioner Association are registered with the Department of Sales Tax and have huge turnovers due to large volumes and have also obtained the licences for carrying on the said business;

(v) that though the purport of the legislations, as enumerated in the Statement of Objects and Reasons is to ban sale/reduce/control sale of cigarettes, tobacco and tobacco products to children admitted in schools but the legislations have also included within their ambit whole sellers when such wholesale outlets are not intended to and do not retail or sell the said products to consumers thereof-that prohibition of wholesale business also within the vicinity of educational institutions is contrary to the basic structure of the said legislations;

(vi) that the business activity of the members of the petitioner can thus cause no harm to the children studying in the educational institutions;

(vii) that the Acts aforesaid, in not differentiating between retail sellers and the whole sellers of tobacco and tobacco products, are arbitrary and in denial of right of livelihood of the members of the petitioner Association;

(viii) that the intent behind the legislations aforesaid is to reduce consumption of cigarette and tobacco products but even if the establishments/shops of the members of the petitioner are shifted to another location beyond the radius of 100 yards from an educational institution, it would in no manner affect the consumption of tobacco and tobacco products;

(ix) that there is no rationale in clubbing whole sellers and retailers together for the purpose of prohibiting sale of tobacco and tobacco products within a radius of 100 yards from an educational institution;

(x) that the same unreasonably restricts the fundamental right to trade, of the members of the petitioner Association, under Article 19(1)(g) of the Constitution of India; and

(xi) that the legislations suffer from the vice of unintelligible classification bearing no nexus with the objectives sought to be achieved there from.

The cause of action for the petitions accrued to the petitioners when in enforcement of the aforesaid Acts, notices were issued to the members of the petitioner Association to stop carrying on their business aforesaid from their establishments within the prohibited radius of educational institutions.

2. Notices of the petitions were issued and vide interim order dated 05.10.2011 in W.P.(C) No. 7292/2011 (challenging the provisions of COTPA), action threatened against the members of the petitioner Association was restrained and the said order has continued in operation till date.

Held by Hon'ble Court

1. We are entirely in agreement with the reasoning aforesaid and find the same to be applicable on all fours to the prohibition in the present case also. Sale of cigarettes and other tobacco products, whether in wholesale or in retail, near the educational institution has the potential of attracting the students thereof and will definitely reduce the access to tobacco. The benefits from the said prohibition far outweigh the harm or loss to the handful of whole sellers. [22]

2. In the facts aforesaid, we find equal treatment of retailers and whole sellers to be having a rational relation to the object of the two legislations and for that matter, other legislations on the subject i.e. to as far as possible prevent exposure of the vulnerable group to tobacco and tobacco products. Moreover, even if there were to be any merit in the contentions of the petitioner with the possibility of students of educational institutions being unaffected by the presence of whole sellers of tobacco and tobacco products within the prohibited radius, we, applying the precautionary principle would rather err on the side of the society at large than on the side of

a handful of members of the petitioner. When a general evil is sought to be suppressed, some martyrs may have to suffer, for the legislature cannot easily make meticulous exceptions and has to proceed on broad categorizations. We therefore dismiss these petitions with costs of ` 20,000/- each payable to the Union of India and Government of NCT of Delhi respectively and to be utilized in appropriate anti-tobacco initiatives.[23]

CHAPTER TWENTY

Utv Software Communications Pvt. Ltd. vs. Union of India and Ors. (10.09.2012 - DELHC) : MANU/DE/4259/2012

Relative Section:
Constitution Of India - Article 19(1)(a)
Hon'bleJudges/Coram:
Hon'ble Mr Justice Rajiv Shakdher
Equivalent Citation: 2012(132)DRJ143
NumberofPagesintheOriginalJudgment:6
Case Reference: nil
Case Note:
Civil- Constitution Of India - Article 19(1)(a) – Writ petition to grant of ex parte stay of the impugned letter dated 02.08.2012; issuance of a direction to respondent no. 3 to consider grant of certification to the film "Heroine" in terms of the provisions of the law which obtained prior to the coming into force of the notification dated 27.10.2011

Direction was also issued to respondent no. 3 to proceed with the certification of the film in issue by taking into account the following two scenarios:

(a). where provisions of clause (ii) of the impugned letter dated 02.08.2012 is enforced; and (b). where the aforementioned provision, i.e., clause (ii) of the letter dated 02.08.2012 is disregarded.

The writ petitioner is concerned, it is averred that it commenced work on the film "Heroine" on 07.06.2011, which got concluded on 13.08.2012.

Facts: Facts, based on which, the writ petitioner has approached this Court, are as follows: -

1 On 18.05.2003, the Parliament enacted the Cigarettes and other Tobacco Products (Prohibition of Advertising and Regulation of Trade and Commerce, Production, Supply and Distribution) Act, 2003 (in short, COPTA Act). The respondent nos.1 and 2 vide notification bearing no. G.S.R. 137 dated 25.02.2004 brought into force certain provisions of COPTA, including section 5, pertaining to ban on advertisements related to cigarettes and other tobacco products. The notification was to come in force w.e.f. 01.05.2004. The rules framed under the COPTA Act known as Cigarettes and other Tobacco Products (Prohibition of Advertising and Regulation of Trade and Commerce, Production, Supply and Distribution) Rules, 2004 (2004 Rules), were also brought in force w.e.f. 01.05.2004 vide notification of even date 25.02.2004.

2 It appears that the 2004 Rules were challenged in April, 2005 in the High Court of Madras, by one, M/s Kasturi and Sons in WP(C) 12344/ 2005. The said writ petition was transferred to this Court by the Supreme Court and consequently, re-registered as WP (C)7411/2006.

3 On 31.05.2005, 2004 Rules were amended. The amended Rules of 2005, inter alia amended Rule 4 of 2004, inasmuch as, it provided for a complete ban on the display of tobacco products and their use in cinema and television programmes.

4 The aforesaid resulted in, M/s Kasturi and Sons, once again, approaching the Madras High Court, in July, 2005, to lay challenge to the 2005 amendment of the Rules. As on the previous occasion, this writ petition was also transferred to this Court, by the Supreme Court, and was re-registered as WP(C) 7410/2006.

5 One, Sh. Mahesh Bhatt, challenged the notification dated 31.05.2005 which, brought about the 2005 amendment to the Rules by filing a writ petition in this Court. The said writ petition was filed on 27.09.2005 and is numbered as WP(C) 18761/2005. The challenge made was directed at insertion of Rule 4 (6) which completely banned the depiction of use of tobacco in cinema and television programmes.

6 On 30.11.2005, the Central Government brought out yet another notification being GSR 698(E). By this notification, which was a second amendment of the rules originally framed, sought to replace Rule 4(6) while seeking to introduce sub rule (6A) and (6B). The notification of 30.11.2005, was also challenged by the said Sh. Mahesh Bhatt, by filing yet another writ petition, in this Court, being: WP(C) 23716/2005. This writ petition was filed on 16.12.2005.

7 On 20.10.2006, vide notification bearing no. GSR 656(E), a third amendment was carried out which sought to incorporate changes in Rule 4. this Court vide order dated 22.02.2006 passed in WP(C) 18761/2005 stayed the implementation of the said notification.

8 On 07.02.2008, a Division Bench of this Court pronounced its judgment in WP(C) Nos. 18761/2005, 23765/2005, 7410/2006 and 7411/ 2006. On account of the fact, that the two learned Judges of this Court presiding on the Bench had deferred on the issue as to whether or not the Rule imposing a ban on use and depiction of tobacco products in Cinema and television programmes was valid or not, the said writ petition was referred to a third Judge. The third Judge vide his judgment dated 23.01.2009, concurred with the view of one of the Judges, by coming to the conclusion that Rule 4 sub rule (6), (6A), (6B) and 8 as finally amended by GSR 656 (E) dated 20.10.2006 were ultra vires Article 19(1)(a) of the Constitution Of India. The said provisions were accordingly struck down. Respondent nos.1 and 2 preferred a special leave petition being : SLP 8439/ 2009. The Supreme Court vide order dated 02.04.2009 stayed the operation of the judgment passed by this Court.

9 To complete the narrative on 27.04.2012, the Supreme Court made an order making the interim order absolute.

Held by Hon'ble Court

1. Given the fact that respondents nos.1 and 2 had taken a decision at the meeting of 29.11.2011 to put certain interim measures in place pending a final decision qua notification dated 27.10.2011, it is prima facie not appropriate for respondent nos.1 and 2 to disturb the state of affairs in the interregnum. This is specially so, as the measures put in place on 29.11.2011 appear to have worked well between December, 2011 and March, 2012. In the instant case, the balance of convenience also appears to be in favour of the writ petitioner in view of the fact that it has invested a huge sum of money based on what was perhaps according to it, was the state of the legal regime, in which, it was required to operate.

2. A substantial part of the film in issue, was completed during the period when the regime put in place vide meeting dated 29.11.2011 held the field. Its withdrawal at the nth hour when, the film is about to be released would in my view be both unfair and detrimental to the interest of the petitioner. Therefore, having regard to the aforesaid circumstances, the following directions are issued :-

(i). respondent no. 3 shall certify the film by marrying the decisions taken in the meeting of 29.11.2011 as contained in paragraphs (ii), (iv)(a) & (b), (v) and the directions contained in para 3(i) of the impugned notification dated 02.08.2012;

(ii). the aforesaid regime shall operate only till such time Respondent nos.1 and 2 places on record a fresh notification superseding all earlier notifications (which I was told includes notification dated 27.10.2011) as conveyed to the Supreme Court at the hearing held on 04.09.2012 in SLP No. 8429-8431/2009, titled tiled Union of India Vs. Mahesh Bhatt and Another.

With the aforesaid directions, the interlocutory application is disposed of.

CHAPTER TWENTY-ONE

Vijay Chandra Jha vs. Delhi High Court and Ors. (11.04.2017 - DELHC) : MANU/DE/0937/2017

Relative Section:

Cigarettes And Other Tobacco Products (prohibition Of Advertisement And Regulation Of Trade And Commerce, Production, Supply And Distribution) Act, 2003 - Section 4, Section 7

Hon'bleJudges/Coram:

G. Rohini, C.J. and Sangita Dhingra Sehgal,

Equivalent Citation: W.P. (C) 10112/2015 and CM Appl. No. 6930/ 2016

NumberofPagesintheOriginalJudgment:2

Case Reference: nil

Case Note:

Civil- writ petition - Cigarettes And Other Tobacco Products (prohibition Of Advertisement And Regulation Of Trade And Commerce, Production, Supply And Distribution) Act, 2003- Permitting and allowing the shop to run inside the court premises is in violation of Section 4 of the Cigarettes and Other Tobacco Products (Prohibition of Advertisement and Regulation of Trade and Commerce, Production, Supply and Distribution) Act, 2003 (for short 'the 2003 Act') as well as Rule 3 of the Prohibition of Smoking in Public Places Rules, 2008 (for short 'the 2008 Rules') made there under.- The relevant statutory provisions. Section 4 of the 2003 Act expressly prohibits smoking in any public place. Section 7 imposes restrictions on trade and commerce in and production, supply and distribution of cigarettes and other tobacco products. Further, Rule 3 of the 2008 Rules provides that the owner, proprietor, manager, supervisor or in-charge of the affairs of a public place shall ensure that no person smokes in the public place under his jurisdiction.

Facts:

1. The petitioner, a practicing advocate, filed this petition as a Public Interest Litigation seeking a direction to remove a shop situated in the premises of High Court of Delhi which is engaged in selling cigarettes.

2. It is pleaded that near Gate No. 7 of the Delhi High Court, there are 15 shops in a row amongst which Shop No. H is a cigarette/tobacco selling shop. It is alleged that the location of the said shop in the High Court premises has led to litigants, advocates, court staff and other people visiting the court to passive smoking and it has also been resulting in people smoking in the small area of glass canteen itself covering the whole area with smoke.

3. It is contended that permitting and allowing the said shop to run inside the court premises is in violation of Section 4 of the Cigarettes and Other Tobacco Products (Prohibition of Advertisement and Regulation of Trade and Commerce, Production, Supply and Distribution) Act, 2003 (for short 'the 2003 Act') as well as Rule 3 of the Prohibition of Smoking in Public Places Rules, 2008 (for short 'the 2008 Rules') made thereunder.

Held by Hon'ble Court

1. In the light of the above-noticed statutory provisions, it appears to us that though there is no absolute bar as such for locating a cigarette selling shop in the premises, it is necessary to ensure that the requirements of sub-section (2) of Section 7 are satisfied. Necessary steps are also required to be taken to enforce the provisions of Rule 3 of the 2008 Rules in the High Court premises.

2. We accordingly direct the Registrar General to place a copy of this order before the Chamber Allotment Committee of Delhi High Court so as to enable the Committee to look into the issue whether Shop No. H which is granted the licence for running a Pan and Beedi can be allowed to continue in the High Court premises.

Adv. Jayprakash Somani's Videos On Law

Adv. Jayprakash Somani's Videos on Law on Youtube- 'jaysomani64' channel.

1) SLP in Supreme Court / Special Leave Petitions in the Supreme Court of India

2) Transfer of Civil & Criminal Cases by the Supreme Court of India / Transfer of Matrimonial Cases

3) Appellate Jurisdiction of the Supreme Court of India

4) Jurisdictions of the Supreme Court of India

5) Public Interest Litigation in the Supreme Court of India / PIL in Supreme Court

6) Article 32 Writ Petitions in the Supreme Court of India

7) Bail Matters Top 10 Supreme Court Cases

8) FIR Quashing in High Court & Supreme Court

9) Bail & Anticipatory Bail Matters in Supreme Court

10) Insolvency & Bankruptcy Matters in the Supreme Court

11) Insolvency & Bankruptcy Code 2016 Part 1

12) Insolvency & Bankruptcy Code 2016 Part 2

13) Insolvency & Bankruptcy Code 2016 Part 3

14) Corporate Liquidation Process

15) Supreme Court Rules & Procedures Webinar of 2.5 hour on Zoom

16) RDDBFI Act, 1993 (Introduction)

17) The Indian Contact Act 1872

18) Negotiable Instruments Act (Introduction)

19) How to avoid matrimonial disputes& some more videos

20) SEBI Matters in the Supreme Court

21) Matrimonial Matters: Supreme Court's 20 Case Laws

22) Consumer Matters Supreme Court's 20 Case Laws

23) Service Matters Supreme Court's 20 Case Laws

24) How to Search Lawyer for Your Matter

25) Property Matters Supreme Court's 20 Case Laws

26) Bail Matters: Supreme Court's 20 Case Laws

27) Supreme Court / High Court Vacation Benches

28) 69000 Teacher's Recruitment Matters of UP Government in the Supreme Court

29) Contempt of Court Matters in the Supreme Court

30) Advocate Act's Matters in the Supreme Court

31) Business Law Matters in the Supreme Court

32) Banking Matters in the Supreme Court

33) Labour Law Matters in the Supreme Court

34) Arbitration Matters in the Supreme Court

35) Careers in Law -Zoom Webinar by Adv. Jayprakash Somani

36) Civil Matters in the Supreme Court

37) Consumer Protection Act | Consumer Matters in the Supreme Court

38) Corporate Matters in the Supreme Court

39) Criminal Matters in the Supreme Court

40) Role of Respondent in the Supreme Court of India

41) Motor Vehicle Accident Matters in Supreme Court with case laws

42) Article 131 Original Suits in Supreme Court

43) PIL in Supreme Court/ Public Interest Litigations in the Supreme Court of India'

44) CAB Citizenship Amendment Bill is not Unconstitutional

45) Supreme Court of India Cases & Process – Marathi

46) Legal Services Export / Export of Legal Services

47) Transfer of Matrimonial Cases by the Supreme Court of India

48) Public Interest Litigation PIL

49) The Specific Relief Act (Introduction)

50) Corporate Insolvency Resolution Process CIRP

51) ABMM's Career 5 - Careers in Law

52) Transfer of cases by Supreme Court

53) Writ Petitions in High Court & Supreme Court of India

54) Supreme Court Jurisdictions - Appeals, SLP, Writ Petitions, Transfer, Original, Review, Curative

55) LEGAL INDIA TV Show: Cases Handled in Supreme Court

56) Corporate Liquidation Process

57) Legal Services Export / Export of Legal Services

58) Corporate Laws

59) Election Matters- Supreme Court's 20 Case Laws

60) Companies Act, 2013

62) Competition Act, 2002

63) Banking Matters - Supreme Court's 20 Case Laws

64) Election Matters in the Supreme Court

65) Armed Forces Tribunal Matters in the Supreme Court

66) Compassionate Appointment Service matter

67) Foreign Exchange Management Act FEMA

68) Foreign Trade Policy 2021-26 Proposed

69) Customs Act 1962

70) Narcotic Drugs and Psychotropic Substances Act, 1985 NDPS Act

71) Foreign Trade Development & Regulation Act, 1992

72) How to Search Good Advocate in the Supreme Court of India

73) Sr. Adv Vikas Singh's Interview in Nani Palkhivala Wednesday Law Club

74) Indian Penal Code (I. P. C.)

75) Criminal Procedure Code (Cr. P. C.)

76) Commercial Courts & International Arbitration - by Mr. Jaideep Gupta, Senior Advocate in Nani Palkhivala Wednesday Law Club

77) Sr. Adv Ranji Thomos in Nani Palkhivala Wednesday Law Club

78) Urgent Matters in Supreme Court during vacations

79) 498A Bail Matters in Supreme Court

81) 376 Bail Matters in Supreme Court

82) 302, 304, 307, 308 Bail Matters in Supreme Court

83) 138, 420 Bail Matters in Supreme Court

84) POCSO Act Bail Matters in Supreme Court

85) NDPS Act Bail Matters in Supreme Court

86) What is ED (Enforcement Directorate)?

87) Prevention of Money Laundering Act, 2002 (PMLA Act)

88) Insolvency & Bankruptcy Code- Supreme Court Case Laws. Webinar in Nani Palkhivala Wednesday Law Club

89) What is NCLT & NCLAT?

90) Acquittal from 376- Supreme Court's some case laws in Nani Palkhivala Wednesday Law Club dt 28.7.22

91) Insolvency & Bankruptcy in India

92) Can we file case directly in the Supreme Court?

93) Adv. Anuja Pethia has cleared AOR Exam 2021 with 77% marks - Her interview in Nani Palkhivala Wednesday Law Club

94) Customs Act - Supreme Court Case Laws & Interview of AOR Adv. Anuja Pethia in Nani Palkhivala Law Club.

95) The Uttar Pradesh Public Service Tribunals Act, 1976

96) POCSO Act - Supreme Court Case Laws & Interview of AOR Adv. Shoumendu Mukharji & Adv. Nishant Verma in Nani Palkhivala Law Club.

97) Who Can Trigger CIRP Process Under Insolvency Law of India

98) The Uttar Pradesh Government Servant Discipline and Appeal Rules, 1999

99) CIRP Application Under Sec 7 by FC

100) Information Technology Act 2000

101) Uttar Pradesh Recruitment of Dependants of Government Servants Dying in Harness Rules, 1974

102) Foreign Exchange Management Act 1999 & Supreme Court's Case Laws on FEMA & Leading Case of AOR Exam in Nani Palkhivala Law Club.

103) Arbitration and Conciliation Act 1996 & It's Supreme Court Case Laws in Nani Palkhivala Wednesday Law Club.

104) Narcotic Drugs & Psychotropic Substances Act 1985 (NDPS Act) & It's Supreme Court Case Laws in Nani Palkhivala Wednesday Law Club.

105) Recovery of Debts and Bankruptcy Act 1993

106) Uttar Pradesh Land Revenue Code 2006

107) CIRP Application Under Sec 9 by OC

108) CIRP Application Under Sec 10 by CD

109) Hindu Succession Act, 1956

110) Maharashtra Civil Services Rules, 1981

111) Indian Contract Act, 1872 & Supreme Court's Case Laws" in Nani Palkhiwala Wednesday Law Club

112) Securities and Exchange Board of India Act, 1992 i. e. SEBI Act 1992 & Case Laws on Insiders Trading" in Nani Palkhiwala Wednesday Law Club

113) Moratorium Under Section 14 of IBC, 2016

114) Hindu Marriage Act, 1955

115) Maharashtra Land Revenue Code, 1966

116) 64 Leading Cases of AOR Exam Session 1 :- Cases 1 to16 in Nani Palkhiwala Wednesday Law Club

117) 64 Leading Cases of AOR Exam Session 2: Cases 17 to 32 in Nani Palkhiwala Wednesday Law Club

118) 64 Leading Cases of AOR Examination Session 3: Cases 33 to 48 in Nani Palkhiwala Wednesday Law Club

119) 64 Leading Cases of AOR Exam Session 4: Cases 49 to 64 in Nani Palkhiwala Wednesday Law Club

120) Labour Laws of India: Part 1 - 4 New Labour Law Codes of India

121) New Labour Laws Part 2 The Code on Wages, 2019

122) New Labour Laws Part 3:- The Code on Social Security, 2020

123) Argue in English Fluently & Confidently - Two months online course.

124) SLP Admission in the Supreme Court. 2023 (Hindi)

125) Transfer of Petitions from the Supreme Court (Hindi)

126) Review Petition in the Supreme Court.(Hindi)

127) Recovery of debts from the Company (Hindi)

128) How to search 'Good Insolvency & Bankruptcy Consultant?' (HINDI)

129) Curative Petition in the Supreme Court

130) AFT Appeals in the Supreme Court (HINDI)

131) NCLAT's Appeals in the Supreme Court.

132) Transfer Petition: Which matters can we transfer?

133) SLP Types of SLP in the Supreme court of India (English).

134) Argue in English Fluently and Confidently in the High Court & Supreme Court'.

List Of Adv. Jayprakash Somani's Published Books

1. Supreme Court of India's Leading Case Laws on 'Insolvency & Bankruptcy Code 2016'

2. Bail Matters – Supreme Court's Latest Leading Case Laws

3. Arbitration Matters- Supreme Court's Latest Leading Case Laws

4. Property Matters - Supreme Court's Latest Leading Case Laws

5. Matrimonial Matters- Supreme Court's Latest Leading Case Laws

6. Election Matters- Supreme Court's Latest Leading Case Laws

7. SEBI Matters- Supreme Court's Latest Leading Case Laws

8. Banking Matters- Supreme Court's Latest Leading Case Laws

9. Service Matters- Supreme Court's Latest Leading Case Laws

10. Contempt of Court Matters- Supreme Court's Latest Leading Case Laws

11. Consumer Protection Matters- Supreme Court's Latest Leading Case Laws

12. Corporate Law- Supreme Court's Latest Leading Case Laws

13. Supreme Court's AOR Exam- Leading Cases

14. Armed Force Tribunal - Supreme Court's Latest Leading Case Laws

15. Acquittal From 376 - Supreme Court's Latest Leading Case Laws

16. Negotiable instrument – Supreme Court's Latest Leading Case Laws

17. Contract Act- Supreme Court's Latest Leading Case Laws

18. Insider trading- Supreme Court's Latest Leading Case Laws

19. Foreign Exchange and Management Act- Supreme Court's Latest Leading Case Laws

20. Income Tax Act- Supreme Court's Latest Leading Case Laws

21. Company Law- Supreme Court's Latest Leading Case Laws

22. Competition & Monopoly Matters- Supreme Court's Latest Leading Case Laws

23. Compassionate Appointment- Service Matters- Supreme Court's Latest Leading Case Laws

24. Compulsory Retirement- Service Matters- Supreme Court's Latest Leading Case Laws

25. Voluntary Retirement- Service Matters- Supreme Court's Latest Leading Case Laws

26. Removal/Dismissal/Termination from Service- Supreme Court's Latest Leading Case Laws

27. Seniority- Service Matter- Supreme Court's Latest Leading Case Laws

28. Promotion- Service Matter- Supreme Court's Latest Leading Case Laws

29. Equal Pay for Equal Work- Service Matter- Supreme Court's Latest Leading Case Laws

30. Condition of Service- Service Matter- Supreme Court's Latest Leading Case Laws

31. Customs Act- Supreme Court's Leading Case Laws

32. Information Technology Act- Supreme Court's Leading Case Laws

33. SEC. 125 CR. P. C.- Supreme Court's Leading Case Laws

34. SEC. 498A OF I. P. C.- Supreme Court's Leading Case Laws

35. MOTOR VEHICLE ACT- Supreme Court's Leading Case Laws

36. CONDITION OF SERVICE- SERVICE MATTER- Supreme Court's Leading Case Laws

37. SUSPENSION- SERVICE MATTER- Supreme Court's Leading Case Laws

38. Reservation in SC, ST, OBC- Service Matter- Supreme Court's Leading Case Laws

39. NARCOTIC DRUGS AND PSYCHOTROPIC SUBSTANCES (NDPS) ACT - Supreme Court of India's Latest Leading Case Laws

40. SEC 302 IPC - Supreme Court of India's Latest Leading Case Laws

41. PROTECTION OF CHILDREN FROM SEXUAL OFFENCES ACT (POCSO) - Supreme Court of India's Latest Leading Case Laws

42. PMLA ACT BAIL MATTERS - Supreme Court of India's Leading Case Laws

43. SEC 376 BAIL MATTERS - Supreme Court of India's Leading Case Laws

44. SEC 302 BAIL MATTERS - Supreme Court of India's Leading Case Laws

45. POCSO ACT BAIL MATTERS - Supreme Court of India's Leading Case Laws

46. JUVENILE JUSTICE ACT- Supreme Court of India's Leading Case Laws

47. TRANSFER OF PROPERTY ACT- Supreme Court of India's Leading Case Laws

48. PROFESSIONAL ETHICS OF ADVOCATES- AOR EXAM- SUPREME COURT'S LEADING CASE LAWS

49. WHITE COLLAR CRIME- SUPREME COURT'S LEADING CASE LAWS

50. SEC 302 BAIL MATTERS- SUPREME COURT'S LEADING CASE LAWS

51. SEC 7 IBC 2016 - SUPREME COURT'S LATEST LEADING CASE LAW

52. ADVERSE POSSESSION IN PROPERTY MATTER - SUPREME COURT'S LATEST LEADING CASE LAWS

53. ARMED FORCE TRIBUNAL ACT- SUPREME COURT'S LATEST LEADING CASE LAWs

54. ESSENTIAL COMMODITIES ACT 1955- SUPREME COURT'S LATEST LEADING CASE LAWS

55. 'FOREIGN TRADE DEVELOPMENT AND REGULATION ACT'- SUPREME COURT AND HIGH COURT'S LEADING CASE LAWS

56. 'PARTNERSHIP ACT 1932'- SUPREME COURT'S LEADING CASE LAWS

Books are available online in India

1. Notion Press: https://notionpress.com/author/jayprakash_somani

2. Amazon: https://www.amazon.in/s?k=jayprakash+somani

3. Flipkart: https://www.flipkart.com/search?q=Jayprakash%20Somani

Books are available online at International Market

4. Amazon International: https://www.amazon.com/s?k=jayprakash+somani

5. Amazon United Kingdom: https://www.amazon.co.uk/s?k=jayprakash+somani

6. E-Books/Kindle edition at National & International Level: https://www.amazon.in/s?k=jaypraksh+somani

Adv Jayprakash Somani's Online Courses

Download our app to get access to our Free Videos, Free Bare Acts, Free Study Material in Legal as well as International Business Regime.

Android App Link ;-https://clpandrea.page.link/cmSm

Ios APp Link :-https://apps.apple.com/us/app/classplus/id1324522260

Login with org code ;- (qywzji)

Web Link ;-https://qywzji.courses.store/

Download App on Google play store - Type

<u>Jayprakash Somani SupremeCourt</u>

Legal Courses :

1. SLP- Bail Matters- Drafting & Successful Arguing in the Supreme Court.

Description - This Course is helpful to Advocates, Litigants, Law Officers, Law Students, Law Schools, Individual. Course contains 8 Videos + Study Material+ PDF Books. Access to this course is for Two Years. Expected duration of this course is one month only.

Topics : 1. SLP- Bail Matters- Drafting & Successful Arguing in the Supreme Court, **2.** Types of bails, **3.** Laws related to bail matters, **4.** How to read Impugned Order of High Court & frame substantial question of laws, **5.** How to draft excellent SLP, **6.** Searching of citations/ case laws, **7.** How to argue in admission hearings, **8.** How argue in after notice hearing.

Speaker: Jayprakash Bansilal Somani, MBA (Foreign Trade), LL. B. Advocate, Supreme Court of India & IP www.jayprakashsomani.com Call: P. A. 9322188701

2. SLP- Succession Matters- Drafting & Successful Arguing in the Supreme Court.

Description - This Course is helpful to Advocates, Litigants, Law Officers, Law Students, Law Schools, Individual. Course contains 9 Videos + Study Material+ PDF Books. Access to this course is for Two Years. Expected duration of this course is one month only.

Topics :1. SLP- Succession Matters- Drafting & Successful Arguing in the Supreme Court, **2.** Information about Succession Matters, **3.** Laws related to Succession Matters, **4.** How to read Impugned Order of High Court to frame substantial questions of law, **5.** How to draft excellent synopsis & list of date, **6.** Drafting of SLP of Succession Matter, **7.** Searching of citations/ case laws, **8.** How to prepare notes & then argue in admission hearings, **9.** How to prepare notes & then argue in after notice final hearing.

Speaker: Jayprakash Bansilal Somani, MBA (Foreign Trade), LL. B. Advocate, Supreme Court of India & IP www.jayprakashsomani.com Call: P. A. 9322188701

3. Legal Vocabulary & its practice pattern to Argue in High Court and Supreme Court / Improve Your Legal English

Description - This Course is helpful to Advocates, Litigants, Law Officers, Law Students, Law Schools, Individual. Course contains 11 Videos + Study Material+ PDF Books. Access to this course is for Two Years. Expected duration of this course is three month only.

Topics : 1. Legal Vocabulary & its practice pattern to Argue in High Court and Supreme Court / Improve Your Legal English, **2.** 1000 legal verbs with its three forms, **3.** Twelve Tenses with its running practice, **4.** One Pdf book on legal vocabulary & its practice pattern with Latin Terms, **5.** Second Pdf book on legal vocabulary & its practice pattern with Latin Terms, **6.** Some Videos of CJI Dr. Dhananjay Chandrachud for the practice of good legal English, **7.** Some Video/Audio Lectures of Legend Nani Palkhivala for standard perfect legal English & flow of Speech, **8.** Some Videos of renowned Sr. Advocates from Mumbai for flow, legal vocabulary & their struggle in legal journey, **9.** Some Videos of Sr. Advocates of the Supreme Court for flow & legal vocabulary, **10.** Some Videos of foreign persons to improve Professional English & thinking process in English, **11.**

Some important legal doctrines with case laws.

Speaker: Jayprakash Bansilal Somani, MBA (Foreign Trade), LL. B. Advocate, Supreme Court of India & IP www.jayprakashsomani.com Call: P. A. 9322188701.

4. SLP- Property Matters - Drafting and Successful Arguing in the Supreme Court.

Description - This Course is helpful to Advocates, Litigants, Law Officers, Law Students, Law Schools 8 Individual. Course contains 9 Videos + Study Material+ PDF Books. Access to this course is for Two Years. Expected duration of this course is one month only.

Topics : 1. SLP- Property Matters - Drafting and Successful Arguing in the Supreme Court, **2.** Types of Property Matters, **3.** Laws related to Property Matters, **4.** How to read Impugned Order of High Court to guide client & frame substantial question of laws, **5.** How to draft Synopsis & List of Dates in Property Matter, **6.** How to draft excellent SLP of Property Matter, **7.** Searching of citations/ case laws with specific paras, **8.** How to argue confidently in admission hearings, **9.** How argue confidently in after notice & final hearings.

Speaker: Jayprakash Bansilal Somani, MBA (Foreign Trade), LL. B. Advocate, Supreme Court of India & IP www.jayprakashsomani.com Call: P. A. 9322188701.

International Business Courses -

1. Agri Products Exports - Scope from India.

Description - This Course is helpful to Agriculturalists, Entrepreneurs, Exporters, Importers, Students. Course contains 12 Videos + Study Material+ PDF Books. Access to this course is for Two Years. Expected duration of this course is one month only.

Topics : 1- Agri Products Exports - Scope from India, **2.** Agri Export's share in India's total export, **3.** Agri Export Promotional Council's Support, **4.** Top 10 Agri export countries, **5.** Top 10 Agri export product, **6.** India's share in World's Agri Exports, **7.** Onion Exports from India, **8.** Rice Exports from India, **9.** Mango Exports from India, **10.** Fresh Vegetable Exports, **11.** Fresh Fruits Exports, **12.** Export of Agri Allied Products.

Speaker: Jayprakash Bansilal Somani, MBA (Foreign Trade), LL. B. Advocate, Supreme Court of India & IP www.jayprakashsomani.com Call: P. A. 9322188701.

2. Textile Exports - Scope from India.

Description - This Course is helpful to Textile Business Houses, Entrepreneurs, Exporters, Importers, Students. Course contains 14 Videos + Study Material+ PDF Books. Access to this course is for Two Years. Expected duration of this course is one month only.

Topics : 1- Textile Exports - Scope from India, **2.** Textile Export's share in India's total exports, **3.** Support of Textile Export Promotional Council, **4.** Top 10 Countries in Textile Exports, **5.** Top 10 Products in Textile Exports, **6.** Export of Readymade Garments, **7.** Export of Man-made Textiles, **8.** Export of Handloom Products, **9.** Export of Wool & Woollen Textiles, **10.** Export of Silk, **11.** Exports of Handicrafts & Carpets, **12.** Exports of Coir & Coir Manufacturers, **13.** Exports of Jute,14. India's share in World's total textile expor.

Speaker: Jayprakash Bansilal Somani, MBA (Foreign Trade), LL. B. Advocate, Supreme Court of India & IP www.jayprakashsomani.com Call: P. A. 9322188701.

3. Export Import Procedure -Perfect Documentation & It's Management.

Description -This Course is helpful to Business Men, Service Providers, Entrepreneurs, Exporters, Importers, Students. Course contains 13 Videos + Study Material+ PDF Books. Access to this course is for Two Years. Expected duration of this course is three months only.

Topics : **1.** Export Import Procedure, Perfect Documentation & Its management, **2.** Company Formation, **3.** Opening of Bank Account in AD Bank, **4.** Export Procedure points, **5.** Import Procedure Points, **6.** Taking Import Export Code, **7.** Taking RCMC number, **8.** Registration at Port when necessary, **9.** Quality Inspection Certificate of Goods, **10.** CHA & its roll, **11.** Custom Formalities, **12.** Export Documents such as Invoice, Bill of Lading, Insurance Certificate, Quality Inspection Certificate & others, **13.** Excellent Management of Export & Imports Documents.

Speaker: Jayprakash Bansilal Somani, MBA (Foreign Trade), LL. B. Advocate, Supreme Court of India & IP www.jayprakashsomani.com Call: P. A. 9322188701.

4. Jewellery Exports -Scope from India

Description - You can understand world wide scope for Jems & Jewellery in multidimensional ways. 14 videos of this course will create positive spark among you to enter into the Exports & Imports of Gems & Jewellery and other products. Chance to ask your query to Somani Sir every week.

Topics :1. Jewellery Exports - Scope from India, **2.** Jewellery Export's share in India's total exports, **3.** Support of Jems & Jewellery Export Promotional Council, **4.** Top 10 Countries in Jewellery Exports, **5.** Top 10 Products in Jewellery Exports, **6.** Export of Cut & Polished Diamonds, **7.** Export of Gold Jewellery, **8.** Export of Plain Gold Jewellery, **9.** Export of Studded Gold Jewellery, **10.** Export of Silver Jewellery, **11.** Exports of Platinum Jewellery, **12.** Exports of Imitation Jewellery, **13.** Exports of Articles of Gold, Silver & others, **14.** India's share in World's total Jewellery export.

Speaker: Jayprakash Bansilal Somani, MBA (Foreign Trade), LL. B. Advocate, Supreme Court of India & IP www.jayprakashsomani.com Call: P. A. 9322188701.

5. Export Import Finance Management with LC, ECGC & Venture Capital.

Description -You can understand A to Z about International Finance with LC, ECGC & Venture Capital in simple language & with illustrations. 11 videos of this course will create positive spark among you regarding International Finance Management with practical tips. Chance to ask your query to Somani Sir every week.

Topics : 1. Export Import Finance Management with LC, ECGC & Venture Capital, **2.** Which is good & excellent source of finance, **3.** Banking Finance, **4.** List of Banks which provides finance for International Business, **5.** How to start business in Less or Zero Capital, **6.** Letter of Credit, **7.** Types of LCs **8.** Scrutiny of L/C, **9.** ECGC Policy, **10.** Venture Capital Finance., **11.** Ideal formula of Investment & continues growth.

Speaker: Jayprakash Bansilal Somani, MBA (Foreign Trade), LL. B. Advocate, Supreme Court of India & IP www.jayprakashsomani.com Call: P. A. 9322188701.

6. Shipping & Logistics in International Business with live links of Ports, ICDs, CHAs etc.

Description - This Course is helpful to any Businessman, Professionals, Entrepreneurs, Exporters, Importers, CHAs, & Students.

Course contains following 10 Videos + Study Material+ PDF Books. Access to this course is for Two Years. Expected duration of this course is three months only.

Topics : 1. Shipping & Logistics in International Business with live links of Ports, ICDs, CHAs etc, **2.** Roll of CHA in Shipping & Logistics of International Business, **3.** How to find good & genuine CHA, **4.** Courier/

post service for small parcel, **5.** India's important Ports & ICDs with live links, **6.** How & what to study Ports/ ICDs websites, **7.** Art to reduce charges of Shipping & logistics, **8.** Information about some Top International Ports with live links, **9.** Roll of Customs in Exports & Imports,**10.** How to become CHA .

Speaker: Jayprakash Bansilal Somani, MBA (Foreign Trade), LL. B. Advocate, Supreme Court of India & IP www.jayprakashsomani.com Call: P. A. 9322188701.

7. International Business Marketing Part 1: Finding Potential & Genuine Buyers for Exports and Suppliers for Imports.

Description -You can understand Seven Excellent ways to Find Potential & Genuine Buyers for Exports and Suppliers for Imports with illustrations. 11 videos of this course will create positive spark among you regarding International Business Marketing with practical tips. Chance to ask your query to Somani Sir every week.

Topics : 1. International Business Marketing Part 1: Finding Potential & Genuine Buyers for Exports and Suppliers for Imports,**2.** Seven Excellent Ways to find Potential Buyers for Exports, **3.** Top 20 B to B Websites in the World, **4.** Searching Potential Buyers from B to B Sites. Is this safe & good way to search potential buyers, **5.** Searching Potential Buyers through Export Promotional Councils & Its Magazines, **6.** Searching Potential Buyers with help from Embassies, **7.** Searching Potential Buyers through Chamber of Commerce at global level, **8.** Searching Potential Buyers from International Trade Fairs & Exhibitions, **9.** Searching Potential Buyers through your friends & relatives or any Indian Person in focus countries, **10.** How to find focus countries for your products or services, **11.** Taking references from establish buyer/seller.

Speaker: Jayprakash Bansilal Somani, MBA (Foreign Trade), LL. B. Advocate, Supreme Court of India & IP www.jayprakashsomani.com Call: P. A. 9322188701.

8. International Business Marketing Part 2: Communication Skill to take repeated orders from Potential Buyers

Description - You can learn Perfect Communication Skills to initiate International Trade with foreign buyers and art to take repeated orders from these Potential Buyers with illustrations. 11 videos of this course will create positive spark among you to reach upto One Star Exporter Level rapidly and subsequent journey to reach upto Five Star Export House. Chance to ask your query to Somani Sir every week.

Topics :1. International Business Marketing Part 2: Communication Skill to take repeated orders from Potential Buyers,**2.** Preparation of Impressive Company Profile, **3.** Excellent Product CatLog for International Market, **4.** Phone Calls with maintaining dignity of ourself & our country, **5.** Sending emails, **6.** Sending what's app messages, **7.** Technique of repeated follow up, **8.** Art of taking 100% advance payments, **9.** Before giving credit facility how to look credibility of potential buyers or suppliers, **10.** Art of earning good profit of margin, **11.** Art of managing international clients.

Speaker: Jayprakash Bansilal Somani, MBA (Foreign Trade), LL. B. Advocate, Supreme Court of India & IP www.jayprakashsomani.com Call: P. A. 9322188701.